T0149586

"Kimberly has opened a portal where Archangels can communicate and teach us how to be powerful sentient beings. The Archangels have important messages for all of us on our evolution of consciousness. I am grateful that Kimberly openly shares these gifts of love and light. Her intimate experiences with her spirituality and her own inner struggles make this book engaging. Offering guidance, methods of clearing energies, insight about spirit guides, and her own experience with her partner Ken make it even more fascinating.

Awakened Empath is a wonderful book for all those that seek spiritual clarity, guidance, and companionship with our evolution and soul's journeys.

Namaste."

— Teza Zialcita, Author of *Universal Conscious Self*

"I often recommend Kim's first book as the "go to" resource for clients who are coming to grips with their empathic abilities. Now I have another resource to further help them along their journey. This is a lovely book, a moving account of a difficult passage, full of heart and wisdom. It is an offering from a true spiritual friend."

— Gerry Gavin, Hay House Bestselling Author of *Messages from Margaret* and *If You Could Talk to an Angel* (www.gerrygavin.com)

"Kim's honest sharing and guidance about life will inspire and lead you to your own spiritual awakening! A must read follow-up to "Waking up an Empath".

— Cathy Anello, Author of *Six Months to Live- Making Each Day Matter*

Awakened Empath

The Evolution
Continues

Sequel to
Waking Up An Empath

Kim Wuirch

BALBOA.
PRESS

A DIVISION OF HAY HOUSE

Balboa Press books may be ordered through booksellers or by contacting:

Balboa Press
A Division of Hay House
1663 Liberty Drive
Bloomington, IN 47403
www.balboapress.com
1 (877) 407-4847

Because of the dynamic nature of the Internet, any web addresses or links contained in this book may have changed since publication and may no longer be valid. The views expressed in this work are solely those of the author and do not necessarily reflect the views of the publisher, and the publisher hereby disclaims any responsibility for them.

The author of this book does not dispense medical advice or prescribe the use of any technique as a form of treatment for physical, emotional, or medical problems without the advice of a physician, either directly or indirectly. The intent of the author is only to offer information of a general nature to help you in your quest for emotional and spiritual well-being. In the event you use any of the information in this book for yourself, which is your constitutional right, the author and the publisher assume no responsibility for your actions.

Any people depicted in stock imagery provided by Thinkstock are models, and such images are being used for illustrative purposes only.
Certain stock imagery © Thinkstock.

Print information available on the last page.

ISBN: 978-1-5043-9100-9 (sc)
ISBN: 978-1-5043-9101-6 (hc)
ISBN: 978-1-5043-9102-3 (e)

Library of Congress Control Number: 2017916943

Balboa Press rev. date: 11/08/2017

DEDICATION

To my only child Seth, I dedicate 10 percent
to you, just because I love you.
Ken, I dedicate 90 percent to you because you are mentioned
throughout the entire book. Also, because I love you. Thank you
for making my continued spiritual journey so remarkable.

CONTENTS

AUTHOR'S NOTE

Are you ready for this book? Archangel Razial says you are. The Writing Archangel that has been helping me write this book says you are.

I strive for accuracy and truth in my writing, even when it makes me feel uncomfortable. Even when it goes against everything I was taught. Even when what I am saying directly contradicts another who is believed to have been right for a long time. Especially if it contradicts what I thought or believed previously. I am still remembering, learning, and seeking, so every day I must update to the present moment.

I would encourage you to read the entire book before you decide anything for yourself. I will not hide behind another and say I am just the messenger, because I don't believe that to be true. I speak for myself and I choose what to say.

My advice to you is simple. Keep updating to the present moment, for this is how you will evolve. Keep healing, for this is how you will increase your vibration. And please, don't let fear stop you from doing either one.

For those of you who are further along the path than others, please be patient with those who are only recently awakening. Remind yourself where you started, so you come from a place of compassion and understanding. We need to teach all levels of understanding and speak in laymen's terms, so as not to exclude anyone. Spirituality is not an exclusive membership. Everyone is invited.

For those who have been part of my journey thus far, thank you for your contribution. I am fortunate to receive so much love and support. I appreciate those of you who have challenged me with your questions and ideas. Everyone who crosses my path provides me with an opportunity to grow in some way and I hope I can do the same for all of you.

Love and Light,
Kim Wuirch

CHAPTER 1

The End

In my last book, I left you with the knowledge that I would be getting married on September 6, 2015, which was, coincidently, the one-year anniversary of my spiritual awakening. That is where this book shall begin, so that you do not miss any part of the journey.

Tyler (whose name I have changed to protect his identity) and I had planned a very elaborate wedding at a significant cost of twenty thousand dollars. I hired all the professional help I would need, including wedding planners. We wanted it to be perfect, of course, as anyone does when they believe they are marrying the person they think they are meant to be with. We hired photographers, a videographer, a caterer, a DJ, and many other people to help. Tyler was interested in the details of the wedding but he knew I was organized and had a talent for event planning, so he left all the important decisions to me.

The planning process was enjoyable for me. I was grateful for the distraction of the wedding, my full-time job, and my spiritual endeavors, because other areas of my personal life seemed to be falling apart. Tyler was having issues running his business and had entered legal battles over money. He seemed to be at odds with business vendors, staff, and even clients. With no direct involvement, there was little I could say or do to help him. Added to that, Tyler was involved in an incident at our engagement party in May 2015, which led to court and lawsuits, so you can imagine the stress levels in my household.

Trouble seemed to find Tyler with ease. So much so that we broke up in July 2015 after I walked out of our shared house. I cancelled the wedding and everything. But then I felt this invisible elastic band snap me right back to him. My emotions ran high and my anxiety higher still until I agreed to work it out and resume the wedding plans. I was baffled to say the least. This was not typical behavior for me. When I decide to do something, I rarely change my mind. Maybe I loved him more than I thought, I rationalized to myself.

The big day arrived on September 6, 2015. It was raining when the limo pulled up to the house to take my wedding party to the ceremony and reception location. I thought everything was perfect, and if it wasn't, it was no longer important.

Upon my arrival, the ceremony was about to begin. Everyone was seated. My son was standing by my side to whisk me down the aisle. I walked slowly but surely along the white carpet, which had been laid out just for me. The lights flashing all around me barely registered as I watched my soon-to-be husband ahead. Finally, I took my place by his side. My veil hung perfectly down my back. My maid of honor adjusted the bottom of my dress but I didn't look at her. The officiant recited the agreed upon words but I heard nothing. Somewhere in the depths of my mind all the words must have registered, as I lifted my hand to have the sapphire and platinum ring placed on my finger.

Next, we were moved to a table to sign the wedding contract. I took my seat and my now-husband stood beside me. Someone placed a pen in my hand and pointed at where I had to sign.

Before the wedding, I had already decided I would not be changing my name. I signed with my full name: *Kimberly-jo Wuirch*

And that's when it happened…

My whole life changed in an instant. The second after I signed my name on that dotted line I was **FREE**. I felt it as clearly as if I had been slapped in the face. Whatever had bound me to Tyler had just been released. That invisible elastic band had disintegrated. I carefully covered my face so as not to show my shock and amazement. I could not tell anyone! In that split-second I knew my marriage was over before it had even begun. But I could not do anything about it. For the remainder of this wedding day I had to hide every thought and emotion I experienced. No one would understand, as even 'I' did not understand exactly what was going on. But one thing I knew for certain, was that somewhere, somehow, I had made an agreement with Tyler that we would marry, and I was bound to that commitment. Once fulfilled, however, I was released from that agreement, and it had happened the moment I signed my name.

During the first dance with my husband, my only thought was, *what am I going to do now that my marriage is over?*

I made it through my wedding day on autopilot. This was certainly not what I expected it to be like. Naturally I wanted to try to make things work between us so I made no immediate move to do anything. I told no one. How could I even begin to explain? Within days it was clear to me that with the release of whatever had taken place, my feelings for Tyler went too. I felt nothing at first. No love, hate, nor anything in between. There was nothing between us. Still, I persisted because I felt that I had made a promise. As the days passed, his anger and depression grated on me.

Then he gave me an ultimatum. He told me to choose between him and my spirituality. He had never shown any interest in my spiritual affairs nor did I expect him to. However, spirituality took up more and more of my time and he became resentful of that. He said it was taking me away from him. I cannot deny that, as it WAS taking me away from him. I had changed and he had not. I understood that. He said if I did not give up the spiritual stuff, I should only do it when he was not around. He asked me to not do it 100 percent of the time and I told him spirituality was 100 percent a part of me, and he could either take it or leave it.

For the first time in my life I had found something that made me truly happy. I had found purpose and meaning in my life. Anyone that wanted to take that away from me was viewed as a threat. That threat rapidly became resentment as I felt judged. Trying to take away my spirituality was like trying to take away my son. I would fight to the death for it.

Our marriage lasted until October 29, 2015, less than two months after taking our vows.

A disagreement turned into a fight, which turned into me asking for a divorce. He moved out of our house and into our cottage where he remained while the separation papers were filed and signed. I sold the house we lived in and moved into a rental house. He remained in the cottage we had built together and I never saw him again.

The end.

Later, I learned that Tyler and I were lovers in a past life and I had made a contract with him before coming to Earth for this lifetime. In that past life I was a man, Tyler was a woman, and we were planning to get married. For some reason, I had to leave and I told him I would make it up to him. I had agreed to marry him, but in that life, something happened and I was unable to fulfill that agreement, so it carried forward in my Akashic Records. Since the agreement was only to get married, once that had been fulfilled, the contract dissolved and there was nothing more to bind us together.

I have since learned that there are better ways to clear contacts, deals, and agreements that no longer serve us from our Akashic Records. I am grateful to have gained this ability, which I use to help my clients so they don't have to go through what I did. I share this knowledge with you later in chapter 20.

CHAPTER 2

The Beginning

On August 4, 2015, a month before my wedding, I received a lunch request via text from a total stranger named Ken who claimed to know my friend Teza and wanted to meet me. I pondered the request before I text messaged Teza and asked, "Do you know this Ken guy and is he some sort of weirdo creeper? He asked to meet me for lunch. Any clue why?"

Teza responded almost immediately, "Ha, Ha! Yes, he's harmless. We were all talking about you at an event yesterday and he just wants to meet you, to know who we were talking about. He's new to the area and doesn't have many friends."

Teza had been in Calgary for another large spirit expo. She was staying at my house again, but I was at work when I received the text from Ken.

I texted Teza back and thanked her. Then I texted Ken back agreeing to meet him at a public place. I was still suspicious of his motives but I didn't tell him that. I chose to meet him a sushi restaurant as it was a favorite of mine. I figured if he harassed me I could always poke him in the eye with a chopstick. Not as good as a sharp stick but I can be resourceful when push comes to shove.

I arrived at the restaurant first and notified the staff that my guest would be arriving shortly. Then I texted Ken to let him know I was already there.

Ken arrived shortly after. He took a seat across from me and we introduced ourselves. I began assessing him in the way I do as an empath. There were no warning signs. He was not a danger to me, but I was not ready to let down my guard yet. He was enthusiastic and curious. I noticed he asked a lot of questions as a way of deflecting any personal questions about himself. He was more than happy to talk about himself, so long as he was the one choosing the topics. I was fine with that and let him chatter away as I listened politely and tried to figure out why we were here.

He seemed to want to impress me but not for the usual reasons. I noticed there was no attraction between us. I found this very curious indeed as I am often deflecting sexual advances from men. Yet this attractive, fit male clearly had no desire for me whatsoever. Even if he tried to hide it, I would have known. I finally decided I must not be his type. So, as he listed his certifications, I wondered why he was trying to impress me with his many qualifications and skills. Then I realized it came from deep insecurities.

He was not grounded at all, which explained why he rambled on constantly without taking a breath. It also explained his hyper behavior. I guess he finally realized he had done most of the talking and had not learned anything about me, so he returned to peppering me with questions. My answers were short and to the point. Then he started grilling me about my spiritual qualifications as a healer. Again, my answers were brief. I still did not know what his motivation was, so I decided not to divulge any more information than necessary.

He asked me to tell him the state of his chakras right there at the table. His experience had probably been that most people were more than willing to prove themselves. But he had never met me before. Unlike other people he may have met, I do not feel the need to prove myself to anyone. The first thing that went through my mind was, if this guy had all these qualifications, why couldn't he assess his own damn chakras? How could he not know his root chakra was totally closed and his sacral chakra was only half functional? Did this guy know anything about spiritual healing at all?

Then came the light bulb moment. I saw through him like saran wrap. It's not that he really wanted me to prove myself at all. It's that he wanted free healing. Now the question was why?

Continuing to play along, I told him, "Your sacral chakra is barely functional and your root is non-functional. You might want to work on that."

He asked if I would clear it for him.

"Sure," I said, "text me later and we can talk about it." I was brushing him off, thinking this was the last time I would see him. He was going on a ten-day meditation the next day and I had a wedding coming up.

Later that day, he texts me asking if I could work on his sacral chakra and root chakra for him. I replied that he could book an appointment with me at a rate of $80 like the rest of my clients. He said he was leaving for his meditation retreat the next day, so that would not be possible. I replied, "See you after the wedding then ☺."

I knew he needed healing, but I would not let anyone devalue my services. Many people do not value a gift unless they give something in exchange. I felt this was true in his case. I did not appreciate the way he expected me to give him something for free with no offer of compensation. We were at a standstill, and honestly, I never expected to hear from him again.

In my mind, I wished him well and hoped his ten-day meditation retreat brought him the healing he so desperately needed.

CHAPTER 3

$$\ast\!\!-\!\!\ast\!\!\ast\!\!-\!\!\ast$$

Deep Healing

To my surprise, I received a text from Ken during my honeymoon asking how I was. I told him I was on my honeymoon and I would get back to him when I had returned to the real world. True to my promise, I did. Tyler and I spent our honeymoon at our nearby cottage, but I needed that time to sort through what had happened at the wedding.

I politely asked Ken about his meditation retreat, but he told me very little. He asked about my wedding and honeymoon, but I told him very little. Then he shocked me and asked if we could exchange healing services. He suggested that we take turns doing healing work on one another as a trade. I thought maybe we would both benefit somehow, so I agreed.

Tyler had planned a hunting trip and was going away for five days, so I told Ken we would have the house, and my healing room, to ourselves to work if he was okay to make the journey from Calgary to Airdrie. My son always came home with me after school and then went to his Dad's for the night, so we set a time after that.

Our first get together was spent coming up with a plan. What healing did we need? What would we work on? What skills did each of us bring to the table? We talked into the wee hours before we realized the time. We had become so consumed by our conversation, that evening turned to night, and night turned to 3 a.m. I rushed Ken out the door and threw myself into bed worried I would be exhausted the next day!

I could not figure out how I had lost track of time like that. One topic had led to another effortlessly, ranging from crystals to channeling to healing.

Our second meeting was to do an assessment on Ken and some basic energy work. Once again, he came to my house and we used my healing room. We chatted for a while and then he hopped up on my Reiki table and I did a Reiki session on him. Very quickly I discovered two tears in his auric field, and one of them was quite significant. I told him this and mentioned he would have felt tired and lethargic lately as he was leaking energy like a sieve. He confirmed this was true. I asked if someone had worked on him recently. We were quite sure it was caused by the last healer he had allowed to work on him. Once the tears were sealed up I attempted to work on his root chakra. I was not able to open this, so I cleared as much as I could. Or rather, as much as his body could handle. He seemed happy with the session and grateful his auric field had been repaired. We chatted a while longer before he left for home, which was rather late again.

Our third session was for me, as we agreed we would take turns. This time Ken was going to take me through a simple past life regression. I had only ever done past life regressions on myself, so I was quite intrigued. His method was rapid regression, which was not my preferred method. I found it too fast, which caused me to feel pressured and stressed. I learned nothing significant. I saw myself just after I had been born, as if I were an observer in the crowd. Then my view changed and I was a baby being held by people with light blue skin who were so happy to see me. I felt the love. Somehow, I knew I had just been born on a planet called Sirius and I was known as a Sirian. The vision quickly faded and I was back in the present, but the feeling of their love for me did not fade so quickly. I wish I had learned more but the whole vision passed so fast.

We were not intending to do healing. Rather, we were testing out each other's skills in these initial sessions. For once we called it an early night.

On our fourth session, I offered to take Ken through a past life regression using a guided meditation taken from one of my Sylvia Browne (Harrison, 2002) books, to show Ken the difference in regressing methods. It was much slower and gentler and just as effective. I asked that when he next took me through a past life regression, that he use this technique with me rather than the rapid regression we did the first time.

The fifth session was for Ken. Once again it involved energy work as he seemed to require a lot of it. His auric field had held up well since I last repaired it. I did more energy clearing on him until his body needed a break. Progress was being made, even if it was slow. Once again, I had no success opening his root chakra. I did notice, however, that he had a habit of trying to leave his body during the healing sessions. I did not stop him; instead I just observed this behavior. It seemed he was not consciously aware of it, so I did not mention it for the time being.

The sixth session is when the preverbal shit hit the fan. On my request, Ken would use the guided meditation I provided to ease me into a trancelike state and allow my mind to regress into a past life. Our intention was to deliberately go back to a time when I needed the most healing. We both understood the meditation would only take us so far and at a certain point Ken would have to use his channeling ability and ask the necessary questions to keep things progressing.

We began with me lying on my back on my Reiki table, with Ken sitting in my comfortably cushioned, leather desk chair nearby. As he read to me, I was lulled into a semi trance by his voice. I knew I was supposed to follow his words but instead I found myself drifting. In my mind, I was already elsewhere, but I was happy and unconcerned. My body got heavy until I no longer felt it anymore. Then I realized Ken had stopped talking and I wondered if I had missed a question.

"What?" I asked

"Where are you?" Ken asked gently

"Oh, I'm not sure actually. There's not much around here, but

I appear to be outdoors. Just a lot of rock and grass, and not much else," I said

"What's your name?" Ken prompted.

"I don't know. I'm a young girl with long hair. The place where I am now, I come to a lot," I replied.

"How old are you?" Ken asked.

"I don't think I know my age, nor does it seem important. Playtime is very important. I come here every day to meet my friends."

"Who are your friends?"

"They aren't human. I'd describe them as fairies and sprites, but there are larger beings too. The larger ones aren't human either, but I don't have a word for what they are. They only meet me here in this place."

"Where is this place?"

I started to feel some resistance now. I didn't want to know this. Why was he pushing me? I did not feel comfortable and I refused to answer the question.

Ken tried again, "Where do you live?"

"Nearby in the village. Our cottage is at the edge, closest to where I am now." I found myself moving towards my cottage and then I was running. Something terrible had happened!

"Noooooo!" I moaned and I started crying. I could no longer hear Ken's voice as a flood of painful memories filled my mind so quickly, before I could even try stop it. In an instant, I remembered everything and I started keening mournfully. My keening turned into wailing and then to guttural sobs that seemed to be never-ending.

The pain and grief was clawing at me from the inside out. I couldn't seem to break free until finally Ken's voice broke through.

"Tell me what happened?" Ken insisted.

"I can't; you wouldn't understand. Unforgivable. I'll never forgive myself. How could I?" I started keening once again.

Unaware of how much time had passed, Ken broke through again. "Tell me anyway!"

I tried, although I was unsure if he understood my words through my crying. "My brother. Dead. I knew the moment it happened but I wasn't there. I ran. I ran so fast, but I was too late. Still, I tried. I didn't want to believe it. I knew where he was. They were still standing there. In the well, just out of reach. Sort of a well. A hole in the ground where we got water. There were rocks around it and we covered it so that animals wouldn't fall in. He was in there. Too deep. I screamed! The other boys said he fell in. Adults are there now. Lying. They LIED! I KNOW WHAT THEY DID!" I started sobbing uncontrollably once again.

I tried again. "The boys were playing and my brother was accidently knocked into the well where he drowned. They were so afraid that when asked what happened, they lied. They said he must have fallen in, but they didn't see what happened. They said they were too late to save him."

I took a breath, "The scene changed to me as an adult. I knew what had happened. My depression had been so great, that I never went back to that place to play. That place is now known as Stonehenge. As a child in that time long-ago, I wasn't just playing inside the great stones. I was learning through play. I was learning how to be the guardian of the portal. Those beings I thought I was playing with were teaching me how to be the guardian under the guise of play. When I saw my adult self, I knew I never went back there among the stones, but I was still the guardian, none the less. Somehow, I'd learned enough to be the guardian as I grew. Since the day my brother died, I blamed myself. If only I had been closer. I'll never leave again. I decided, and I never did.

"Then, that fateful day in which the portal was breached. I felt the breach in the portal the moment it happened and I was unable to stop it. Once breached, I knew they'd destroy it, and then they'd go after the guardian. I knew they were coming. Perhaps if I'd continued my training this never would have happened. I believed I failed as guardian. I was sure they'd kill anyone to get to me. To prevent anyone else I loved from dying, I felt I knew what I had to do. With my two children inside, I took two steps outside the cottage I grew up in. I threw up my arms in surrender, and within moments the possessed man on the horse rode by, slicing open my throat with his sword. My last sacrifice as guardian."

In the present, my crying persisted more quietly now as I rocked myself, hating myself for being such a failure to mankind. "I never went back. Not in all the thousands of years I've incarnated here, I never went back. I'm so sorry. So very sorry I failed in my duty."

Ken was quiet. I was so lost in my own emotions that for once I could not read his reaction. Then he spoke softly. "There's someone here who wants to talk to you. He says he's a Sirian from the Federation of light. He hasn't spoken to humans in a thousand years."

All I could do was nod that I was listening.

Ken continued to channel the Sirian being. "We understand what happened and we do not blame you. We do not think your sacrifice was necessary. We forgive you. We forgave you long ago. Now you must forgive yourself. This is of the utmost importance. Do not let what happened before affect you now, for this you cannot change."

"How can I forgive myself for something so unforgivable?" I questioned.

"Do it not yourself but for them," the Sirian said through Ken. "He's gone now." Ken told me. "However, there are some angels here that want to say something." Ken was clearly not used to talking to angels. "They said to tell you, they forgive you, too."

This only made me cry harder.

I told Ken I wanted to go to bed. It had been a rough night and I was exhausted. I was not yet able to come to terms with any of what had gone on. I asked Ken to keep everything that had happened confidential. "I will," he promised. "Who would believe me anyway?"

Good point.

The next day Ken asked me how I was doing. Not great, to be honest. I was sullen and sad and wondered what I could have done differently. Then it occurred to me. It was not about me. I didn't need to forgive myself for me because it was not about me. I needed to forgive myself and move on, because whatever was on the horizon, is what mattered. Not what I did or didn't do in the past. Not what I couldn't stop.

It may sound too crazy to be true, but part of the reason I held off writing this second book for so long is because I was not sure if the world was ready to hear my side of the story. Or if anyone would believe it.

I cannot control what people think, so I have let go of any attachment to the outcome. The important thing to me is that I healed something within me that was broken for a very, very long time. I will be forever grateful to Ken for helping me heal that part of me and that part of my history.

Oh, and by the way, the boy who died, my younger brother...

That was Ken.

CHAPTER 4

Oh My Aching Back

After Teza taught me how to open my Akashic Records, one of my very first questions to the keepers of the Akashic Records was, "Will my back be healed in this lifetime?" The answer I got was, "Yes."

I felt excited about this because I had been born with scoliosis, a chronic and debilitating disease that twists your spine. In my case, my spine was shaped like an 'S.' As a young tween, I cried myself to sleep when I had growing pains because my misshapen spine would interfere with the process. At age 18, I had nearly constant lower back pain. It was not until the age of 22 that I got a full-time job with benefits and went to see my first chiropractor. She discovered I had scar tissue fusing the skin of my lower back directly to my spine. As she pulled my skin away from my spine, it was not the popping noise that got my attention so much as the severe pain! I will be forever grateful to her for that, because my constant lower back pain ceased after that. From then on, I only had occasional lower back pain. Most of the issues after that were in my upper back, ribs and neck.

My spine would twist when it felt like it with no rhyme or reason. My ribs would pop painfully out of place and need to be manipulated back to where they belonged. The muscle spasms would cause me to lose my breath and I would often wish I did not have to breathe at all. When I was pregnant with my son, my back must not have had the proper room it needed to twist because somehow my tailbone managed to curl inward making sitting down the most painful experience ever.

To get a yes to my question about my back being healed in this lifetime was a dream come true. I didn't know when. I didn't know how. But I had hope. I assumed someone else was going to heal it for me and I could not help but wonder if maybe it was this John of God (John of God, 2017) I had heard about. Perhaps I needed to save money for a trip to Brasilia, the capital city of Brazil. I had heard about his miraculous healings and thought perhaps he was my only hope.

After another healing session on Ken, it was my turn again. I was not interested in another past life regression. Not yet anyway, as I was still recovering from the last one.

We were chatting about the options and possibilities when Ken was signaled by an archangel. We both became quiet as we tried to decipher the message. There was an archangel surgeon, a Sirian surgeon, and a couple of others who told us they could help me heal my back, but that they needed to work through my hands to do it and they needed permission. Then I was shown a vision of doing Reiki on myself and holding my hands there until the process was complete. Ken was told to pay attention for any additional instructions and channel any information as provided, but otherwise he had to stay back and not interfere in the process.

Once again, I was lying on my back on my Reiki table. Ken was once again in my leather desk chair nearby with his eyes closed, focused, in case he was given more instructions.

My hands hovered over my mid-section and I felt the energy coming through them as it always does when I do Reiki. I gave permission for this team to assist me in any way possible and we began. It started off as a slow heat building in my body. I was getting warm, then warmer, then hot until I started to sweat a little. I felt a pinch. Then a twinge. I started to pant slightly.

Then time lost all meaning.

The pain was hot and fast, ripping through my spine with ferocity. My body arched. Ken reminded me to keep my hands where they were. "No matter what," he said, "keep your hands where they are." He didn't need to tell me. I would give anything to have my back healed and no amount of pain would prevent me from getting what I wanted the most.

White hot pain blazed through me and my body twisted. I howled in pain, as my back wracked with spasms. My body moved of its own accord, into unnatural positions, twisting and knotting. The tears flowed. My hair was matted to my face. My clothing was soaked and clinging to my body. Guttural sounds came from my mouth that I did not recognize as my own.

Then it was over.

I did not know how much time had passed, but I felt so weary I could not keep my eyes open. Exhaustion was claiming me quickly. Ken muttered something but it sounded muffled to me. I may have dozed off. Eventually, Ken helped me off the table and saw himself out. I do not remember changing into pajamas but I woke up in them, so I must have. I was out before I hit the pillow.

For three weeks, I felt bruised and sore and achy. I started to think it had not worked. How could I be feel sore if I was healed? I certainly didn't feel healed.

However, after those three weeks, the most amazing thing happened. I felt good. Really good! My back did not hurt at all. Weeks turned into months. It was six months before my back needed to make a shift again and only because it was still healing. It only lasted a week or so and then months passed again before the next shift.

My back has never twisted again. It may not be straight but it is a luxury to me that the pain of the twisting is gone.

Thank you, Sirian Surgeon. Thank you, Archangel Tushit (first known to me as the Archangel Surgeon). Thank you everyone else who assisted.

One day I will find a way to repay you for this great debt of service.

Months later, I discovered that the origin of my scoliosis was from a combination of two past lives. In one past life, I was tortured and killed, and in the other I had a debilitating illness.

Unfortunately, I saw the one where I was tortured and killed. It started out in a courtyard. Nothing fancy – in fact, much like you might see in the movies where everyone meets to exchange goods and the ground is nothing but dirt. I think there were horses milling around and there was straw scattered on the ground.

Somehow, I had angered the crowd, or perhaps they had been looking for me. I was a young girl, probably between the ages of 16 and 22. People were yelling and calling me a witch. Then I was being pelted with stones. The crowd closed in on me until two men grabbed me and dragged me out, but not to save me. They dragged me until we reached some steep stone steps and then I was unceremoniously tossed down them. At the bottom, I barely caught my breath as I sat up, gasping. Then I was grabbed again and tossed into an underground cell. For good measure, I was kicked in the ribs and I felt/heard the crack of my ribs breaking. Sadly, I don't think I ever recovered. My broken body lay there helplessly, as I slowly blacked out.

The illness I suffered from in a different lifetime did not kill me, so I'm told. I do not know what the illness was or how it contributed to my scoliosis in this lifetime.

CHAPTER 5

Root Chakra

In November 2015, my life was in turmoil. I had separated from my husband. He had taken all his possessions and left me to get the house sold. This was no small under-taking as it was not a small house and between us we had a lot of things. I also needed to find another place to live. I had meetings with lawyers, real estate agents, a job to do, and a child to look after. On such short notice, I didn't have many options for help and I was not ready to explain to people why I was separating after only two months of marriage. So, I asked my new friend Ken who, as it happened, was not employed and had lots of free time. He was my saving grace. Not only did he help me pack an entire house, drop off donations, clean and sort, he also didn't ask a lot of questions. He earned my respect with his quiet support and non-judgement, which meant a great deal to me.

Everything happened so quickly that it seemed like it was meant to be. All the paperwork went through without a hitch. The house sold in three weeks and was finalized in six weeks. The first rental property I looked at was exactly the right one and I loved the landlord. Pets were not an issue and I could move in early. I had just enough money to pay all the deposits and get by until the money from the house was settled. Ken offered his large van to help move all my breakable belongings and I hired a moving company for the rest. In the blink of an eye I was moved and settled. My life had completely changed yet again.

Somehow, while all of this was happening, Ken and I continued to have our agreed upon sessions, taking turns to work on each other to heal and develop our abilities. While my house was in turmoil we agreed that taking our sessions to his house would be much easier. The first time I arrived I observed a non-descript neighborhood. A modest, low income, two-bedroom apartment with sparse furnishings that was clean and bright. Ken shared his apartment with his daughter and their cat.

He did not have a healing room like I did, so we decided to set up in the living room. I immediately cleared the space, lit candles and prepared it until I felt it was ready for spiritual healing work. We threw some cushions and blankets on the floor for Ken to lie on, and I sat nearby on a pillow.

"Today is the day I'm going to open your root chakra," I stated

"Great!" Ken replied.

"Just so you know, I have no idea how this is going to work. I'm going to figure it out as we go," I said.

"I'm okay with that," Ken said with a smirk.

I started off with some relaxation techniques. This bought me some time as I tried to figure out what to do. I continued to guide him into a past life regression, and I directed him to go to the moment his root chakra had closed. As I spoke, I did some energy work over his root and sacral chakra, which were not budging an inch. He kept trying to avoid going to the time when his root chakra had closed, so I directed him to go back to a few days before his root chakra closed. He did and found himself in his mother's womb.

As we fast forwarded slowly, he tried to leave his body, except this time I did not allow it and I put my hand on the crown of his head, preventing him from getting away. When I questioned, what had happened while he was in the womb he started to cry so hard I could not understand him. I continued to keep one hand on his crown chakra and I used the other to pat his shoulder as I murmured words of comfort. I had to keep reminding him that he was safe and he was only to observe. His body seemed to be reliving whatever trauma took place no matter how hard I tried to put in him the observer's seat. His body was shaking so hard I worried he might go into shock, so I directed him to go into another timeline. I told him there was a timeline in which none of this had happened. I said, "Go there and experience what it could have been like if no trauma occurred." He did so and relaxed immediately. Then I directed him to bring back everything that was good about that timeline while he was in the womb and his birth. Somehow, I was directed to integrate the experience and make it part of this timeline for him. Though afterward I could not remember how I did it.

By the time we were done, two hours had passed. When I checked on his sacral chakra, I was pleasantly surprised to find it was open and functional. I proceeded to his root chakra and I was stunned to find that open and clear too. I gave Ken the good news, and while he looked completely bedraggled, he was also relieved. To give him some space to gather himself, I packed up the items I had brought with me and blew out the candles.

What happened next felt surreal.

I asked Ken how he was feeling, which drew his attention to me and we made eye contact from across the room.

CRACK

It was not an external noise so much as the air crackled.

It was like I was seeing him for the first time and the attraction hit me full force. I knew that Ken was having the same experience, because he could not hide his erection through the loose shorts he was wearing. I watched as his eyes widened, his face turned red, and he turned towards the fridge to open it as if he wanted something cold. I never took my eyes off him.

Until that moment neither of us had felt an ounce of attraction for one another. Finally, he turned back to face me. I had not moved a muscle.

"I guess I can't really hide it, but I don't know what happened?" Ken said, clearly embarrassed.

"I don't know either, but if it makes you feel any better, the same thing happened to me. Girls are just lucky that we can hide it better," I said, smiling.

That made him laugh.

"What's really odd is that from the first time I met you I thought you were attractive. Yet I was not 'attracted' to you, which I found strange. I kept asking my guides, 'why am I not attracted to her? She's hot, after all.' I never got an answer, except that after I asked twenty times they finally told me to stop asking," Ken said.

I found this quite funny. "Well I never questioned why I wasn't attracted to you. As far as I was concerned, I was getting married and if you so much a move in my direction I'd have bolted in an instant. Yet I still found myself wondering why you never hit on me or showed any interest at all," I said, still laughing

"And now things have changed," Ken stated.

"And now things have changed," I repeated.

"Interesting," Ken said.

"Very," I replied.

As tempting as it was to act on this change, we didn't. Not immediately anyway. Honestly, we felt more confused than anything. I needed some time to figure out what had just happened.

We never figured out what really happened or why. Our guides seem to be tight-lipped about the whole thing. It makes me wonder what their involvement was.

What is even more interesting is how Ken came to be living in Calgary in the first place. You see, my awakening happened in September 2014, over a long weekend. Coincidently, right after that long weekend, Ken had the sudden urge to move. He didn't know where to move to so he pulled up google maps on his phone and kept zooming out until he saw the city he needed to move to. Calgary. Without knowing why but feeling an urge so strong he could not ignore it, he and his daughter moved to Calgary. This was during the boom so getting a rental property at that time was near impossible. Competition was fierce and options were limited. Yet by some miracle Ken found an apartment almost immediately.

Ken and his daughter were moved and fully settled in Calgary by October 1, 2014.

For fun, Ken found his moving announcement from Facebook, so I could share the story in his own words. Dated Oct 10, 2014:

"Super cool synchronicity/serendipity story!

(For reference, Calgary is probably one of the hardest places in the world to find a place to rent because of the hot economy.)

I heard in my spirit to move to Calgary, so I found a place online. The guy told me they were doing a showing at 7 p.m. the next day. So, I drove down early to go "pound the pavement" before my meeting. I stopped at a friend's place and he showed me a map of Calgary and all the good areas. He kept offering for me to use his laptop to look for places online, but I kept hearing in my spirit, to just "go out there." So that's what I did and here's what happened.

I went to the community I wanted to live in. I drove past a guy raking his leaves. I backed up and asked him if he knew any place for rent in the community. He told me he didn't but that I should go across the street and talk to Steve in the red house. So, I talked to Steve but he didn't know of any rentals either. As we were talking, two ladies were strolling by with their kids. Steve asked them if they knew of any rental properties and one of them said her mom had a place for rent and said to follow her.

I followed her to her mom's house and her mom told me she had two places available for November. I told her I needed a place right away. "In that case," she said, "you need to talk to Stacy who has an apartment down the street." I called Stacy and left a message. Stacy called back shortly after and said she had two places available for October 1. Two days later, I drove back with my damage deposit.

All of this happened within three days. Talk about synchronicity and serendipity. I feel so blessed."

CHAPTER 6

Sirian Guides

My friend sent me an email with a link for a channeled message that she thought might interest me. The message was to have been channeled from a Sirian, so naturally this caught my attention knowing I had at least one life on this star called Sirius. I read through it and it was vaguely interesting, but nothing about it seemed to resonate strongly with me. Then I got to the bottom where it said who the channeled message came from and I saw the name:

SaLuSa

The tears flowed fast and the words that came out of my mouth were, "my friend."

It's rather disconcerting to be crying without knowing why, let alone why you would call someone your friend who you never remember meeting. But I had met him. I knew SaLuSa, as we were close at one time and I missed him the very moment I heard his name.

It is hard to explain the emotion and the knowing I felt. I know not everyone will understand or believe me, and that's fine. It was not until months later that I told Ken about SaLuSa. When I spoke of him, he came right away and Ken got to "meet" him by channeling him. SaLuSa confirmed for Ken that he and I were friends long ago. He said hi to me and then he left again.

It seemed natural to me that I had such a strong connection with Sirians as I knew I had incarnated there at some point in my history. So far, I had met the Sirian surgeon, the Sirian from the Federation of Light, and now SaLuSa, who was the only one I had a name for. So, it was no surprise when I met my new Sirian guide shortly thereafter.

I was lying in bed chatting on the phone with Ken and asking if he liked my first book, *Waking Up An Empath*, which at the time had not yet been published. I had finished writing it, but I was not ready to publish. Ken had been told by his guide and mine that he really needed to read my book, so I assumed he had read at least half of it. He said he liked it and was reading it, and then I heard a loud "OW!" from the other end.

"What happened?" I asked.

"Someone just poked me in the brain!" he responded.

This made me laugh, because I suspected why he got poked. "Have you been reading my book?" I asked.

"Well, I've been trying but I've felt so tired lately, so I've only read a couple of chapters."

"Uh huh, so who poked you?" I laughed.

"Your Sirian guide. A female. So 'she' poked me. Hey! Why did you poke me?" he said, sounding indignant on the other end of the line.

This made me laugh harder, of course. "Probably because you were told to read the book and you're avoiding it. Get reading, mister. I'm going to sleep," I said as I yawned.

"Okay, I'm reading now. Tell your female Sirian guide to back off! Good night," he said before he hung up.

I didn't tell her to back off, though. Instead, I laughed and told her I thought it was funny as heck and to keep an eye on him and make sure he reads it since it seemed to be so important.

It wasn't long before we discovered my female Sirian guide's strongest ability. She seemed to have a real talent for manipulating electricity. It was HOW I found out that still makes me laugh to this day.

Ken, Teza, and I were all doing an expo out in the Edmonton

region, so the three of us were staying with a friend of mine who lived in the area. Teza had gone out with some friends for dinner, so Ken and I did our own thing. We were driving back to my friend's place when Ken started telling me about the last time he went to an expo a few months prior. He had met a sound healer who recorded a personalized disk for his clients to take home and listen to for the sole purpose of healing. Ken thought this was a great idea and paid to have a disk made for him. He didn't get to listen to the disk until later when he was driving and he put the disk into the CD player of his vehicle.

This is how he described it.

"I put the disk in, all ready to hear soothing, healing sounds, but what came out of the speakers sounded like a cat in a car engine! I couldn't understand it. I thought it was supposed to be calming, but it kept going on like that. Screeching and wailing. It was so high-pitched I thought my ears were going to bleed," he said.

"So, did you turn it off and take it back?" I asked.

"Not exactly," he replied. "I thought maybe it'd still be healing for me since it was made for me and maybe I needed to tough it out longer."

This sounded like the stupidest thing I had ever heard in my life, so naturally I started laughing. He kept going though.

"It was such a horrid sound but I paid a lot of money for it so I wasn't giving up."

As he was describing it to me, his face scrunched up and started turning red. I was laughing harder now.

"Finally, I couldn't take it anymore and I pulled over and ripped the CD out of the CD player and snapped it in two. I was so tense and stressed by this point," he said.

Something was niggling at me while he was telling his story. Then I realized it was my female Sirian guide. Uh oh, I thought. "Did you have something to do with why Ken's CD did not turn out properly?" I asked her in my head.

I swear, I could feel her smiling. Then she showed me what she did in a vision. I saw her go into the machine like a ghost and manipulate the flow of electricity. Then she came out with a smug look on her face. Well, that was it for me. I howled with laughter. I tried to tell Ken what she did but I could barely talk as the tears of mirth rolled down my face. Ken kept looking over at me quizzically, but I could not get the whole story out, for every time I recounted it I laughed even more. As we came to a stop I rolled out of the vehicle and threw myself against the side of the van. I could barely breathe. I knew I might even pee my pants if I didn't get ahold of myself. Except when I tried again to tell Ken what truly happened, I ended up on the ground, rolling around in laughter all over again.

Finally, I managed to spit it out and tell him the whole story. For some reason, he did not find it nearly as funny as I did. I had to wonder if my female Sirian guide and Ken were siblings at some point, because they sure acted like it, the way they were always bickering.

There was also another time when the two of us had some fun with Ken.

Ken had been out of work for a while, so he took the first job that came up where he could start right away. It was doing roofing work on a city apartment building. There was not much parking available so he had snuck in behind someone to park inside the building that you would normally need a pass to get into. He figured he would follow someone in, and at the end of the day when someone went in or out, he would sneak in on foot to get his vehicle again.

I met him there at the end of the day and I had planned to follow him home in his vehicle. He saw me arrive and came over to tell me his parking situation, that he had to wait for someone to go in or come out before we could leave. He ran over to stand by the garage door and wait, while I waited in my vehicle and watched.

After about five minutes my impatience kicked in.

I called for my Sirian guide. "Could you open that garage door for him so that we can leave please? We could be waiting here all night at this rate." I didn't hear a response but in about ten seconds I saw the garage door open. Then I saw Ken looking around with a confused look on his face. Before it closed again, he rushed in and drove out with his vehicle, pulling up beside my Toyota Rav.

"I don't get it," he said, "the garage door just seemed to open all on its own. No one came in or out and no one was around."

I giggled. "I asked my Sirian guide to open it so we could go. Say thank you."

"Oh, I should have known. Thank you," he muttered.

Sadly, she was only with me for a few months before she moved on and was no longer my guide. I struggled to understand why. I didn't want her to go but I was informed I did not need her anymore and someone else would take her place. I did not know who right away. She came back a couple more times because I kept calling for her, but eventually she stopped.

It was explained to me that Sirians are souls, just like humans, only less dense. She was not omnipresent and could only be in one place at a time, and she was busy with other tasks now. I did stop calling her but I never stopped missing her.

CHAPTER 7

Spiritual Abilities

Ken and I have very different abilities and we became aware of this very quickly. At this point, Ken had spent eight years honing his channeling ability, which became his strongest gift. His second strongest ability is clairaudience, which means "clear hearing." This means he can communicate with non-physical beings in his mind.

To channel is to allow other worldly beings to speak through you. For Ken to channel he has to give permission to allow a soul or being to use him as an intermediary to deliver a message. He needs to be in a state of allowing. The key difference is that he uses his clairaudience to get messages for himself, and he uses his channeling ability to pass messages on to others. This is very powerful in and of itself, yet he seemed to lack in many other areas of spirituality.

Strangely enough, I seemed stronger in all other areas of spirituality. Yet my weakest ability, at the time, was my clairaudience. I didn't do any channeling because I refused to allow anyone to speak "through" me. I permitted other worldly beings to speak to me using clairaudience, but I drew the line at channeling. I didn't have a reason, per se, I just felt it wasn't for me. For this reason, I was more than happy to let Ken do all the channeling.

It was only natural for the two of us to learn everything we could from one another and we would spend hours doing exactly that.

First, I taught Ken about crystals and their various uses. I could never remember the names of the crystals, but I didn't need to know the names to feel and utilize the energy they emitted. Ken was extremely skeptical that crystals could do anything useful, which made me laugh. I started off by having him close his eyes, and then I would place a crystal in his hand and ask him what the energy felt like. I tested him with everything from grounding crystals to charged and amplified crystals. He was sensitive enough that he always felt something and I enjoyed the surprise that lit up his face with each new discovery. I let him keep the obvious favorites, which he pocketed quickly.

One night, I set my large quartz crystal ball on the floor and surrounded it with crystals in six straight lines extending out from the crystal ball, and then a circle of crystals on the outer edge. Then I took my Reiki wand and starting at the center, hovering over the crystal ball, I followed a path of crystals. It didn't matter what pattern, I simply moved my Reiki wand so it passed over every single crystal. Then I told Ken to hold his hands above it as if he were warming his hands over a campfire. He couldn't believe the cool energy pumping off the crystals on the floor. He was a believer now!

From there I graduated him to Usui Reiki and getting his first Reiki attunement. He was fascinated that energy now came out of his hands and he could use it for healing and other purposes. He had to follow the same pace as my other students for receiving his attunements and he had to take the training the same as everyone else. I was adamant about that. If he wanted to be trained as a healer, he was going to do it right. Eventually he did learn all levels of Reiki from Usui to Violet Flame, and more from me.

I really put him to the test when I challenged him about whom he was channeling and the accuracy of his messages.

He was shocked the first time I questioned him, which was very clear from the look on his face.

"I have a message for you," Ken said.

"Oh yeah?" I said.

"Do you want to hear it?" Ken asked, as if he was holding in a big secret.

"Sure. What is it?" I asked, playing along.

"I'm supposed to tell you that you need to meditate more and you should practice channeling," Ken said smirking.

"Is that so? Well, isn't that interesting. Who is this message from exactly?" I asked, knowing he would not have an answer.

"What do you mean? That's what I was supposed to tell you. I'm just the messenger," Ken said, getting a little flustered.

"Well," I said, matter of fact, "that's not good enough for me. See, if you're going to give me messages, then you better know where it's coming from. This might come as a shock to you, but just because you get messages from spirits, that doesn't mean they all have our best interests in mind. I don't take advice from just anybody who tells me what to do, dead or alive, spirit or otherwise. So, as I asked before, who gave you this message?"

"I guess I don't know. How would I know?" he asked.

"Well you can ask for a name but that doesn't really help. Nice to have but rather useless in determining intent. You can ask if they're my guide or your guide but they can lie about that. However, there's one thing they can't lie about," I said smiling, because now I had the secret.

"What?!" Ken asked.

"What percentage of the Light they are. No one in spirit form seems to be able to lie about that. All archangels are 100 percent of the light. If whomever you are talking to claims to be an archangel, you should always ask what percentage of the Light they are. If they give you a lesser number than 100 percent, then you know they were lying and you can disregard whatever they told you," I told him.

"Okay, so what if they aren't an archangel, nor are they claiming to be an archangel. Then what do I ask?" Ken asked reasonably.

"Well, that's trickier. The only thing I have found to work for sure is to banish anyone that isn't serving your highest and greatest good (I explain how in chapter 8). Send them away, basically. If you do that and then try channeling and they have disappeared, you know they were up to no good. Otherwise they never would have been banished. See, the idea is that if they're there for your highest and greatest good, they'll still be there after you do the banishment. Then you know whatever they talk to you about you should pay attention to. At least until you learn to discern the difference between your guides and any other souls that just want to chat."

After this conversation, we got curious as to what percentage of the Light angels were. We thought it would be fun to know if we were communicating with an angel, archangel or someone claiming to be one of the above. This is what we learned:

Archangels are 100 percent of the light

Angels are anywhere from 66.6%-99.9 percent of the light

CHAPTER 8

Banishment Spell

I wrote down the banishment spell that I came up with for Ken to use whenever he needed it. Then I shared it with my friends to try out. The results were astonishing. Everyone said how they felt the change immediately. I put the spell on my blog and titled it "banishment spell," as a joke for my friends.

Some people took that title quite seriously, because I was not allowed to post it on certain Facebook pages as it had the word 'spell' in it. The administrators must have assumed it was witchcraft. I refused to change the title just to be politically correct. Those who followed my instructions, also got results, which I was happy about.

I will share it with you here:

"Sometimes we **consciously** or **unconsciously** give permission to souls or beings who simply no longer need access to us. This permission could have been granted in this lifetime or any lifetimes before; it doesn't matter. This command is written in such a way that you cannot and will not revoke access to any soul or being that IS working in your highest and greatest good.

Read the following **out loud.** Make sure you put a lot of meaning and power behind it or else it won't work! Say it three times to make sure you were successful. Do not change the wording, and I cannot stress enough that you must really **mean it** and put power behind your words. Find a place where you do not feel self-conscious about almost yelling it! You won't know if you needed to do it until after. If you notice a difference then it was needed.

'I hereby evict, revoke access, rescind approval to all souls or beings that have access to my being who are not serving my highest and greatest good in all timelines, dimensions, and realities.
ALL souls or beings that are NOT serving my highest and greatest good – GET OUT NOW. All souls and beings that I gave approval to consciously or unconsciously that are not serving my highest good are hereby banned from my presence and my being in all timelines, dimensions, and realities. BY MY WILL SO IT IS!'

I promise you this command works well. You are in control of your body and soul. All I am doing is giving you a tool that allows you to enforce it."

Since I shared this command, I started receiving a lot of requests for how to get souls or beings out of people's homes. Now while I would prefer that you try to help them to cross over to the astral realm, some are simply not willing to do that. Or they are harassing the tenants of the home, in which case I totally understand if you wish to evict them. I have modified the language for exactly this purpose, and it will bring no harm to the souls/beings but it will exit them from the premises.

> *"I hereby evict, revoke access, rescind approval to all souls or beings that have access to my home and the vicinity, that are not serving my highest and greatest good in all timelines, dimensions, and realities. ALL souls or beings that are NOT serving my highest and greatest good – GET OUT NOW. BY MY WILL SO IT IS!"*

CHAPTER 9

Souls

By the time I had met Ken, I was used to souls popping in and out of my healing sessions with clients, and coming and going whenever they felt like it. For the most part they didn't bother me. Unless they specifically asked for my help, I mostly ignored them. Although, they made it hard to ignore them when they were flickering the lights while I was trying to watch TV.

I would see them, smell them, or feel their presence. To talk to them required a lot of concentration on my part. Once Ken was around it seemed he could interpret what they wanted much faster so and I didn't have to work as hard at it anymore.

One time, I was eating breakfast at the kitchen table and Ken was eight feet away making his own breakfast at the counter. Out of nowhere I smelled men's cologne. It was odd because no one had moved, the windows were closed, and I hadn't smelled it before. I was fairly certain Ken didn't wear cologne.

"Ken? Are you wearing cologne? Or did you just put on deodorant or something?" I asked.

He turned to me with a quizzical look on his face. "No. Why do you ask?"

"Because I can smell men's cologne. It's quite distinct and it's coming from right beside me."

He stopped what he was doing and closed his eyes to focus

inwardly. A minute later his eyes popped open. "You need to banish them now. Whoever it is used to know you and they aren't healthy for you. Get rid of him!" Ken said quickly.

I immediately did as he suggested. I was glad I had spoken up about the smell, because lost souls can affect a living person, especially an empath. If the lost soul is very angry or distraught then of course the empath picks up on those emotions and is influenced by them. I sent him away with my banishment spell, and the smell of cologne went with him. I never learned why he was there or how he found me.

Another time, Ken and I were lying on our bed chatting away about a past life that I had remembered. The details were still vague but it seems I was an advisor to a very powerful man. I suspected I lived in China at the time based on the clothing I saw, which was very unusual. I asked Ken if he could ask what era it was. We were not able to get an exact date but we were told it was thousands of years ago in ancient China. While we were talking, I sensed a presence. My body stiffened, because it felt like another lost soul. I alerted Ken immediately. The lost soul told Ken he had a message for me. We checked with our guides if it was safe to talk to this soul and they said it was. Our conversation about my past life seemed to have alerted this lost soul somehow.

The lost soul explained he was an emperor and that I had been his advisor and best friend. He said he died before he could give me a message, so he had waited, not crossing over until he delivered his message to me. Ken agreed to be the channel and let the emperor speak through him. I made a deal with the lost soul that if I listened to his message, he must then cross over, to which he agreed. I listened attentively and politely. What came across, however, were completely nonsensical, meaningless words. He was not making any sense at all! Yet it seemed so urgent to him that I receive this message.

It made me so sad to know this poor man had waited for thousands of years to give me a message, and in waiting he had clearly gone crazy. My response to him was this: "Thank you, my dear friend, for relaying this very important message to me. I have received it now. Please go in peace with this angel who wishes to see you cross as much as I do. It's safe for you to go with them, I promise you this. Goodbye, my friend."

This seemed to appease him and he went. I thanked the female angel that assisted him. I kept my composure until the moment I felt his presence leave, and then I cried. I cried for my friend who should have been in peace all this time, but instead was trapped between the physical plane and the astral realm, which had clearly caused his madness. That's when I understood the importance of ALL souls crossing over. I knew then and there, I would always help any souls should they need it.

All lost souls are simply people who couldn't find their path home. Sometimes they don't go where they are supposed to out of fear or guilt. Or they don't go because they have an urgent message to deliver, yet they don't seem to understand that they can still give us messages after they cross to the astral realm. The challenge is that they have freewill, so no one will force them to go. Sadly, its frequently unhealthy human beliefs that keep them trapped in this in-between state, which I think is commonly known as purgatory in human language. It's almost like sitting on a bridge where you cannot go back the way you came and you don't want to cross the bridge either, because you aren't sure what's on the other side.

These poor souls are not something to fear, as so many of us have been taught through movies and books. They may be sad or angry. They may lash out in their fear and grief. Nonetheless, they deserve love and compassion. If they lash out at us we can banish them for our own safety of course, and that sends them a safe distance away from us. No harm comes to them and if the banishment is not permanent they can come back later. And yes, you can choose to make it permanent.

There is one very special angel who helps these souls cross, however I do not know her name. When she is unable to get these souls to cross over, we may call in the soul family of the lost soul. Depending on the mental capacity of the lost soul, this often works well.

The more we truly understand the truth about what happens after our bodies give out, the less chance there will be of us becoming lost. I want to be very clear when I say this. On the other side of that bridge is love, healing, and your soul family. There is nothing to fear. I know this because an angel told me.

When your time comes, please cross that bridge when you reach it.

There are souls who visit who are not lost and do cross to the astral realm; Ken's dad being one of them. On occasion, souls we knew in a current lifetime cross over and become one of our Earth guides. This was true for Ken. After his dad passed he acted as a guide for Ken for many years. Ken now has other guides, as he has surpassed what his dad could do for him, but, his dad still visits from time to time just to say hi.

On one such winter evening, Ken and I were sitting on the sofa watching TV when his dad showed up. I don't know what made me think of it but I asked his dad if he would like me to light a candle for him and the answer I got was 'yes.' I did so, of course, and then I asked him what the candle did for him? Did it help to anchor him here? No, I was told, it helped him to focus on us.

I thought that was very interesting indeed.

I asked the angels and archangels if lighting a candle helps them focus on us as well and they confirmed that yes, it does. They appreciate an open flame and moving water. Since then I have always tried to incorporate both the elements of fire and water while doing spiritual work.

Incarnated beings like us have earth guides, also known as spirit guides, who have chosen to be our guides while we are here on earth. They are souls like you and I who have personality traits just as we do. Your earth guides could be anyone. They could be someone you've known from this lifetime, someone you've known from a previous lifetime, or someone you've never incarnated with before.

There are two types of earth guides: "secondary guides" who reside on the peripheral and step in to assist from time-to-time, and your "primary guide" who is the one who works with you most of the time.

Typically, you will have one or two that stay with you from birth and the others come and go as needed as you evolve and grow. You can have one guide that can be with you for your whole lifetime, or you can have a guide that is with you for a "season" of your life. When that season is over, that guide will step back and a new one will step forward. When the next season is complete, that guide will step back, and a new one will step forward, and so on. You can have one guide that is with you for your whole life or many throughout your lifetime. There is no right or wrong, better or worse.

On occasion an angel may assist a human and act as a temporary guide which is where the term "Guardian Angel" comes from. It's easy to get angels confused with earth guides. Whomever is helping you, they are there to support you. Being an earth guide is a difficult job, so be sure to show your gratitude as they work hard to keep you on your desired path.

Your primary earth guide is a part of your soul family, also known as a soul group. A soul family is just as it sounds; a family of souls that choose to be together. When not incarnated they reside in the astral realm. When someone transitions from this lifetime (i.e. dies), their soul family will be there to welcome them back. The astral realm is where we reside when we are in-between incarnations.

Just because someone is part of your earth family, does not mean they are automatically part of your soul family. Someone from your soul family could be your aunt, sibling, mother, father, grandparent, cousin, or they could be a friend, teacher or co-worker. Generally, you'll have a strong connection with them and it will seem like you've known them forever. But just because you have a strong connection with someone or feel like you've known them forever, doesn't automatically mean they are part of your soul family. That strong connection you feel, can be a sense of familiarity if you have incarnated with that person many times before.

Because your earth guides have had multiple names over many lifetimes, often they won't give you a name. If you've known them from this lifetime, they may be OK with letting you know it's Uncle Joey. If they give you a name, you should use it and not nickname them. Treat your earth guides with respect as you would expect to be treated yourself.

Your earth guides have a choice of whether they will present themselves as either a male energy or a female energy and they will choose based on how you can relate best to them. The same goes with how they are clothed. People who are clairvoyant (psychic sight) can often see their earth guides attire. People who are clairalience (psychic smelling) might be able to smell when their guides are near, like a familiar perfume or cologne, soap or any scent that would remind you of someone you knew. People who are clairsentient (psychic feeling), will sense their earth guides energy and personality. Earth guides can present themselves as any age, demographic or nationality.

It is important to emphasize that these souls *choose* to be our earth guides. It is a difficult task for them. Many humans either ignore their earth guides or simply don't know what their earth guides are trying to tell them. Since you have free will, you can choose to ignore your earth guides and do your own thing. It may not turn out as you had intended in the long run but you made the choice. If you choose to follow the guidance from your earth guides to the best of your ability, you have a better chance of gaining the growth your soul desires. This does not mean there won't be challenges but rather you will get what you came here for, which is soul evolution.

Your earth guides do all this because they love you. All of them have your highest and best interest in mind. All of them know your souls desire and can help guide you in a way that will help your being evolve to its fullest potential. It simply takes practice learning to decipher what they are trying to tell you.

CHAPTER 10

━━━━━✦━━━✦━━━━━

One Week

My spiritual development process has not been easy. I have been pushed to my limits physically, mentally, emotionally, and spiritually. I have gone through extreme highs and lows. To give you some insight, I will take you through one week in the life of a developing healer/empath/psychic (me).

Welcome to my crazy life.

Day 1

What a great day! The sun is shining. The birds are chirping. I feel amazing. I am so connected with All That Is. It's so easy to connect with my guides now.

I had such an awesome session with a client. I could easily do ten more sessions today! I can't believe I ever struggled to get messages. I'm in flow! My visions are so clear, the words come with ease, and even the healing energy that comes through my hands feels strong. I feel powerful and in-tune with All That Is. I am One with everything!

"Ken, let's book more sessions with people and teach some workshops. We can change the world!"

Day 2

Ugh. What time is it? I am so tired! I don't want to get up. Stupid birds woke me up. Argh! The sun is so bright. Who opened the friggen blinds this early in the morning!

I feel disconnected. I'm so alone! My guides have abandoned me. What did I do? What have I done to be cut off? I'm exhausted. I feel achy. Maybe I am getting sick?

I will have to rebook the client session scheduled today. I can't do a session with someone if I can't get any information. What if that's it and I am never able to do healing work again? I feel so out of sync.

I tell Ken, "I think I'm coming down with something, and I have no connection to anyone, including Razial."

That night I cry myself to sleep and have weird dreams.

Day 3

Wake up at 7 a.m. Ken asks if I am sick.

"No, I'm not sick! Don't be ridiculous. I'm perfectly healthy. I don't know where you got the idea that I was sick," I say, matter of factly. "Come on, we have lots to do today! Some angels were here this morning with some brilliant ideas. Let's go! We have work to do! Awesome, it's a rainy day! A perfect day to stay inside and work with the angels. They have some things they want to share with us."

We spend the entire day channeling and documenting what we learn.

When our brains cannot take anymore, I still have tons of energy, so I clean the whole house, mow the lawn, walk the dog, and bake a cake.

Day 4

What a crappy sleep. It's all Ken's fault. He woke me during the night. I must go to work today and I am exhausted. Great, I got coffee on my white shirt! Fan-freaking-tastic!

Traffic sucks. Probably because no one knows how to drive around here. Bunch of jerks.

Why is everyone in such a pissy mood today? Like it's all my fault?! I can't wait to go home.

Finally, I am home. No one made supper? I am starving, I worked all day, and I come home to an empty house and no supper. I can't take this anymore. I take care of everyone else but where is everyone when I need someone to take care of me?

The crying begins, and once the dam breaks, the flood comes. There's no stopping the uncontrollable sobbing until it abates on its own. Then I sleep like the dead.

Day 5

Me: I'm sick for sure this time. I have the flu. I am dying for sure. I have plague-like symptoms. This could be worse than the flu.

Ken: You're not sick from an illness. You're just going through changes to increase your spiritual abilities and your body is clearing and detoxing itself.

Me: How would you know? You don't even care. I should probably be at the hospital. You'll be sorry when I'm gone.

Ken: Razial says you're fine. It will pass. It's all part of the process. You're not sick and you're not dying.

Me: Fine! I'm not dying. I just wish I were dead. You guys should be more compassionate about my feelings you know. This isn't easy for me. *sniff* I bet I had the plague in a past life and this is what it felt like.

Ken: *rolling his eyes*

Me: I saw that! If you're not part of the solution you're part of the problem! You can go now!

Day 6

Me: That wasn't so bad! I told you I could handle these changes! I say, bring it on. I can handle whatever is thrown my way. I'm tough like that, you know. Like a mosquito bite. A little itchy and annoying but it doesn't last. Clearly, I am built for this stuff.

Ken: Glad to hear it! I'm supposed to tell you that was phase 1, part 1. There are at least three phases but I'm not clear how many parts to each phase.

Me: F*%@

Ken: Would you be upset if I moved out when part 2 starts?

All I had was a pillow within reach to throw at him. Why is there never a heavy object around when you need one?

Day 7

What a great day! The sun is shining. The birds are chirping. I feel amazing. I am so connected with All That Is. It's so easy to connect with my guides now.

Life is perfect once again.

****

Welcome to the rollercoaster that is my ongoing spiritual awakening, healing, and growth.

Seriously though, the changes I have had to endure have been difficult, in much the same way a pregnancy can be difficult for a woman. When a woman is pregnant we go through physical and hormonal changes. We experience emotional mood swings. Our bones soften and spread to make room for the baby. We may become increasingly forgetful.

At least all of that happened to me when I was pregnant with my son, Seth. My body changed from familiar to unfamiliar. What I could see of it anyway. Labor was painful and somewhat scary. Then, when I gave birth, I knew it was all worth it and nothing that had happened prior mattered anymore.

I find that the changes I have experienced up until now, and continue to experience, as a result of my spiritual awakening and development, are very similar to pregnancy.

I go through phases where my brain is being developed or rewired. This causes brain fog, confusion, and forgetfulness. I think? I can't quite remember?

My body must realign itself to allow the proper flow of energy, which means on occasion I can feel my bones softening and moving. It feels strangest in my skull. Almost as though an entire ocean of water is pressing in on my body, only it doesn't hurt. The shifting of my bones is very uncomfortable, even though it happens very slowly. My muscles are pulled in unison.

Exhaustion is the toughest to manage, though. There are days when it does not matter how much I sleep, and I work a full-time job, so that can be challenging. I could be fine all day and then out of the blue, I'll be drop dead tired for what seems like no reason! It can last days or weeks. Typically, increases in my spiritual abilities, spiritual being, and energetic being are directly correlated to tiredness.

In the early phases of my spiritual growth I would get "colds" or "flus," but Razial would say I was not sick. It is all part of the changing and detoxing. Unless I did not get a sore throat it sure seemed like a cold or flu to me! I always get a sore throat when I am sick, so when I had the other symptoms (achiness, runny nose, headache, nausea) and no sore throat, I was more inclined to believe Razial.

The weirdest symptom I ever experienced, was the sudden onset of vertigo. One second I was fine; the next I was dizzy. A minute later it was like nothing ever happened.

When I am not experiencing any of this I feel amazing! Healthy as a horse and tons of energy. To be fair, on my worst day I seem to have more energy than most people. No one can figure out how I manage to work a full-time IT job, and then go home and do the family thing. In addition to that; I see clients for spiritual healing, I do book signings, I develop new healing products, and I facilitate workshops.

It helps that I do what I love. It also shows that getting healthier is worth the time I invested.

CHAPTER 11

Random Important Details

Totem animals:

When I wrote my first book I had a totem animal who appeared to me as a wolf and went by the name of Julia. Since then I discovered my primary totem animal has always been a male snowy white owl named Odin who has a funny sense of humor. My secondary totem animals only stay for a short time until I no longer need their assistance and then another totem animal takes their place. After Julia moved on, a shy little female fox named Lipir took her place.

What I learned from Odin is that totem animals provide us with something we need help with. In Odin's case, his primary ability was to bring me awareness. He showed me a vision of himself sitting up somewhere high and he had a greater perspective from that view. He said he had a "bird's-eye view" from that vantage point. Then he laughed at his own joke. He always laughs at his owns jokes. I swear he is his own best audience. Perhaps we share that in common.

I struggled to figure out what his name was so I asked him to spell it for Ken. Ken would say the letter and I would write it down. L…R…F…N. LRFN? Huh? That's a name? Then I heard him laughing away. Cheeky bird. Give us the right spelling! O…D…I…N. Odin.

Lipir, who is a fox, brings something entirely different. Her major ability is "bridging space." I have yet to figure out what that means.

It's hard to get much information from her because she rarely comes close due to her shyness. Ironic really.

At the time, Ken had a totem animal that looked like a black panther only her fur seemed to have a tinge of cobalt blue in it. Unusual, but very pretty. I could always see her, but Ken only ever felt or heard her. She has since moved on and Ken has not met his new totem yet.

Archangel Metatron seems to know most about them. He says they live in a different plane of existence called realms that overlaps with our own, and that sprites exist with totem animals there. Other than that, I don't know much more about them. I have only ever seen a sprite once as it zipped by, leaving a sparkly trail.

I have heard sprites are very mischievous, so they probably get along quite well with Odin.

Two types of energy:

As an energy healer, it was important for me to understand how energy is channeled through my body. It was explained that there are two types of energy. These are the terms I use but I know others use different terminology. Use your preferred language… you will still get the idea.

1. CHI (also known as Ki, Qi or Prana). CHI comes from our Energetic Being. It is located below the solar plexus and above the belly button. It is used for healing. The amount of CHI that can be generated is dependent on our overall health.
2. Source energy. This is not generated by us, but rather it comes from outside of us. It is used for activations, healing, and a by-product of that is raising our vibration.

Moonlight:

In my first book, I believe I mentioned charging all my crystals in the moonlight. Every full moon I would gently gather up all my crystals and take them outside to lay them out carefully on my back deck. I would have to use laundry baskets to carry them all because I had so many.

Then one day I was playing fifty questions with Razial, and I quickly learned that a lot what I had been taught was not entirely accurate. I asked, "Is it true that crystals are charged in the moonlight?" The answer I got back was, no. "WHAT?!" I exclaimed.

I felt silly now. For at least a year I had been faithfully putting all my crystals out all for nothing. Then I thought, SO WHAT?! Who cares what I was doing before? I did what I thought was right, until I knew better, then I updated my information. I simply needed to update to the NOW. I didn't want to get stuck in my ways, unwilling to change out of pride. If the information I had wasn't correct, then so be it. I know now and that's what's important. That's how we evolve. If we didn't we would probably still think the earth was flat.

So instead of dwelling on what I did wrong, I asked what is the best way to charge my crystals now. Reiki, I was told, was the ideal method for clearing and charging. There are other ways, but since I was attuned to channel energy, Razial told me to use this method.

Individual Intuition: (also known as your Higher Self)

Everyone has individual intuition, although not everyone accesses it. I have been informed that this will start to change very soon. Razial confirms that what some call their Higher Self, is also their individual intuition. Your individual intuition resides in your etheric self. It is like a smaller database that is easily accessible, if you try. Information can be uploaded or downloaded as needed. You see, your brain can only hold so much data. What is not immediately needed is uploaded to your individual intuition and is readily available if one attempts to access it.

Universal Consciousness: (also known as Collective Consciousness)

The universal consciousness is like a shared database. All souls from the Universe feed information into this database. Think of it as a joining of all individual intuition. Everyone can access it. Therefore, you may have heard of scientists from one side of the world who had this brilliant idea, and then they find out that someone from the other side of the world had the same idea. Once it has been added to the universal consciousness it's accessible by anyone who is seeking that same information.

The Void (also known as the gap):

There is a place called the void (or gap by some). It is not a shared space. The void is a space accessible by each individual for the purpose of healing and rejuvenation. No one else can enter your void space, not even your guides. It is easily accessed with intention while in meditation, by simply choosing to go there. Imagine a doorway that you walk through and on the other side will be pure darkness, black as night. You are safe there. It might feel as though you are floating. You can go there as often as you like for as long as you like. Again, no one else can enter, not even archangels. You will be completely alone, completely safe and when you chose to leave you will do so instantly. Entering your void space during meditations will be one of the best ways to advance your spiritual and personal development.

Realms, Realities and Dimensions:

Realms:

Realms are places where only souls reside (no beings). There are three realms where souls reside when they are not incarnated.

The first realm is called The Astral Realm. This is where your soul family resides and where you exist in-between lives. This is where your soul develops and evolves when it's not incarnated.

The second realm is called Purgatory. When humans die suddenly they may become disoriented. When this happens, they may not go all the way to the Astral Realm out of fear or confusion. Their soul remains in-between the astral realm and our physical existence. We often refer to them as, "lost souls" because Purgatory is not where they belong. They belong, in the astral realm.

The third realm is what I call the Spirit Realm, which is where totem/spirit animals reside. When an animal on this physical plane transitions (i.e. your pet), they will go to an aspect of this realm where totem/spirit animals reside. Some totem/spirit animals have abilities that can help humans. If you have a totem/spirit animal that has chosen to help you, treat them with love and gratitude like you would a close friend.

It is possible for souls in all three realms to interact with different realities.

Realities:

Realities exist simultaneously in the space in-between, within our 4th dimension.

A visual example would be to imagine infinite sheets of tinted glass standing vertically. We call these veils. To many of us in this reality, those veils seem dark and hard to see through. However, there are some people who can see psychically see into different realities as though the veils were not tinted at all.

Only in the 4th dimension are there multiple realities. No other realities exist in any of the other dimensions. Realities are where other beings (who do not have souls) live. Some examples are sprites, fairies, and dragons. A dragon, for example, may think that only their reality exists. They may have no idea that there are infinite realities that exist on either side of them. Like humans, they can learn to peer through the veils with practice. Whereas sprites and fairies, who are naturally gifted at transcending realities, will frequently enter our reality and interact with humans or animals. Because they vibrate at a different frequency, some humans who have strong clairvoyant abilities may see them. Humans can pop into different realities from time-to-time unknowingly. With practice, this can be done intentionally.

Dimensions:

You have probably heard of a three-dimensional shape; length, width, and height. Those are the first three dimensions. The 4th dimension is known by scientists as time and space, but time and distance would be a more accurate description. Humans have a basic understanding of the 4th dimension. Most of it is beyond human comprehension. Your physical being resides in the first three dimensions and partially in the 4th. All the remaining aspects of a human (i.e. spiritual, mental, emotional, energetic) reside in the 4th dimension.

There are 12 dimensions in total. There is a 13th dimension but it's not exactly a dimension by the same definition. It's the part that surrounds and encompasses all other 12 dimensions. Angels reside primarily in the 11th dimension and somewhat in the 12th dimension. Archangels, who are the only omnipresent beings (can be multiple places simultaneously) reside primarily in the 12th dimension. Archangels are the only beings who can transcend all dimensions.

CHAPTER 12

Archangel Razial

Just for you Razial, I am going to spell your name the way you prefer in my book. Even though I almost always write it 'Raziel' the rest of the time. I still think it looks better spelt with an E and it has been written that way by humans for a long time!

I didn't become aware that Archangel Razial was my guide until I was flipping through a spiritual book and I saw his name. I stared at the name for some time. Something seemed to be very familiar about it. Then someone jabbed me in the chin. "Hey!" I exclaimed. "What was that for? Ow!" It didn't hurt but I like to be dramatic sometimes.

Ken had been sitting at the table with me and looked up. "What?" he asked.

"I was just reading and someone jabbed me in the chin," I said, sounding indignant.

Ken went quiet for a minute. "It's Archangel Michael. He's trying to tell you something about what you're reading."

"The only thing I found that caught my eye was this Archangel Razial mentioned here. Why do I know that name?" I asked.

"That's it. That's what he's trying to tell you. You know Archangel Razial. You two are very close but you've just forgotten. You need to remember now. It's important," Ken said.

"I wish it were that easy," I said in a pouty voice. "Well, if it helps, Razial I welcome you into my home and into my space. I ask that you help me remember," I said. It felt right and easy. I trusted Razial immediately.

From that day on I ran everything past Razial. I asked endless questions and he was always so patient with me. But that didn't mean he would always answer my questions. Some questions were met with complete silence, which annoyed me at first. Ken would joke that Razial would have his arms crossed in a way that said, "Nope, I'm not answering that." Occasionally, he would not answer because it was not the right question, and other times it was not the right time for him to divulge the information.

When souls or beings showed up to give Ken or I a message, I quickly got into the habit of asking if they were "Razial approved." If Razial said no, I would banish them. If Razial said yes, I would listen to what they had to say. I found this to be an excellent way to prevent getting misinformation, no matter how well intentioned it was. Souls try to help but they certainly don't have access to the bigger picture like archangels do. If an archangel tells me something, I am definitely going to listen.

Sometimes, other people would tell me, "Oh I have a message for you from my guides." I would ask Razial, yay or nay? More often than not it was nay. I would still listen politely to their message and thank them for passing it on, and then two seconds later I would completely dismiss it.

I thought Razial knew everything! Until I asked a question one day and he didn't know the answer. I was stunned when he said he was not the right one to ask and he redirected me to another archangel. I realized I had gotten very attached to Razial. Almost too dependent. I felt like he was sending me away. Not true, he said.

He showed me that even though it seemed like he had only recently come into my life, the truth was he had always been watching over me. He reminded me of specific times he was there, often with other archangels.

When I was 15, I was being pulled behind a skidoo in a sled by a friend along the edge of a frozen river in spring. We took a sharp turn around a bend in the river and the sled swung out sharply and

I was thrown toward the center of the river where the ice was thin and the river was deep. The driver did not notice immediately. I stood up and started walking, pondering why I had not fallen through the ice. I should have. I would have weighed approximately 59 kilograms (130 pounds) at the time. I should have fallen through and because the weather that day was easily -15 Celsius (5 degrees Fahrenheit) or colder, I would have gotten hypothermia. Possibly even died. Yet, I didn't. Another five minutes passed before the driver realized he had lost me and turned around to retrieve me.

Another time, still aged 15, I was a passenger on a motorbike and the driver thought it would be fun to do some wheelies in the sand. The bike spun 180 degrees a few times before I was thrown free, unhurt. Unfortunately, the 100-kilogram (220-pound) driver of the bike lost control, sending the bike in one direction and him in my direction, feet first. Adrenaline made time seem as if it had slowed down. I watched as the heel of his steel-toed, black, leather work boot came towards me and connected with my temple. Light burst in front of my eyes. A minute later, I shook it off with a mild headache. How? I do not know. With his weight, size, and the distance/speed with which he travelled when he connected with the side of my head, I felt sure I would be dead. I never suffered a concussion, a bruise, or any injury.

When I was 12 or 13 years old I was playing with my brothers in the backyard, and for some reason I was trying to get myself higher up a tree. As I am 1.5 meters (5'2) tall, I'm used to having to stand on things so that I can reach. My brilliant idea was to place a cut tree stump on the ground vertically and another vertically on top of that one so the two cut tree logs meant for the fire pit could raise me at least .9 meters (3 feet) higher. Then I climbed up to stand on the top. However, it was not the most stable arrangement and the second log rocked and tipped out from under me, moving my feet outwardly with it. My head crashed down directly onto the first vertical log that remained in place. I felt my brain bounce off the inside of my skull. I would have dropped approximately 2 meters (6 feet). I now understand the cartoons where they see little birdies flying around their heads, as I also saw birdies. It took a few minutes for my aching head to clear but once it did I was fine. I figured I got lucky that time. What I didn't realize at the time was that I should have had a concussion, at minimum, if not severe brain damage.

At age 9, I didn't want to go to bed. I wanted to stay up with the adults so I came to my mom complaining of a mild belly ache on my right side. It was not bothering me that much but I figured it would get me out of bedtime. My mother became extremely concerned about the location I put my hand when I said I had a tummy ache, which was low and to the right. To my utter surprise, I was rushed to the hospital and from there put in an ambulance and rushed to another hospital. I could not understand what all the fuss was about and I regretted trying to get out of bedtime. I enjoyed the company of the EMS tech beside me though. He teased me about going through a drive-thru for a burger. Next thing I knew, I was being put under to have my appendix removed. I hardly felt any pain until after the surgery. It was not until years later that I learned just how painful an inflamed appendix really is and how dangerous it could be if it burst. I didn't suffer or whine, yet somehow my mom still knew there was a danger. I later learned my guide told her.

I was approximately one year of age and in my crib when my mom had the urge to check on me, and did so. When she opened the bedroom door the heat radiating from my small body hit her full force. My fever was high, yet I was standing in my crib with a smile on my face, not the least bit bothered. My temperature was 104.5F. I spent the next ten days in hospital, because a family member was also sick and they didn't want to risk further exposure.

Poor Razial obviously had his hands full with me growing up. My fascination with speed. The fact I never feared death. My constant risk-taking. Illness. He must have been relieved when I got pregnant. From that day forward there was someone counting on me and I refused to take any risks no matter how small. I don't know exactly how Razial or anyone one else helped me in those situations I told you about, but I do know they helped save my life at least five times and they prevented serious injury on several more occasions. That would explain why I have never had a broken bone. This whole time I just thought I was made of rubber. He said they only intervened during life or death situations or anything that would have drastically taken me off my intended path.

He really was my guardian angel.

It was not that easy for me to communicate with Razial at first. Communication was sporadic and irregular. Without Ken's help, I would not have learned as much as I did so quickly. Razial was also testing out various forms of communication with me to determine what would be the most effective for both of us.

I recall being in a salt bath spa, where you lie down in a bath that has pounds of salt dissolved into the water, so you float. You're in a sort of dome covered bathtub where you can close the lid if you want, turn off the lights and music, and meditate. During this experience, I said out loud to Razial that this might create an ideal opportunity for us to practice our communication with each other. Everything was quiet and dark, and I just drifted in suspension. No thoughts. Just calm silence.

CLANG!

I bolted upright so startled because it was like someone had just smashed two pot lids together in my head! My hands flew to either side of my head as I attempted to keep my brains from leaking out of my ears! "What the hell was that?!" I said angrily. I knew it was Razial but I got no answer. I was so shaken up that I climbed out of the bath and got dressed. Ken had been floating in the room next to mine so when he came out I told him what had happened. "What did he do that for?!" I asked Ken.

Ken checked in with Razial. "He said he didn't know it would be that loud for you. He was testing out ways of getting your attention."

"Well he got my attention alright. I think I had a mini stroke in there! Let's NOT use that method," I said, still annoyed.

It's funny now, of course, but at the time I was not a happy camper.

Back to my original point, once I started conversing with Razial on a regular basis I learned that each of the archangels have different perspectives and knowledge. When he told me another angel or archangel could better answer one of my questions, he wasn't sending me away. He just knew someone else was better qualified to answer or assist me.

CHAPTER 13

The A-Team

The information in this chapter is most likely different than much of what you have been previously taught about angels and archangels. I'm not implying that I am right and other teachers are wrong. Rather, I believe we, as a human race, were simply not ready for this information before now. Perhaps we were told what we were ready to hear and the information relayed to Ken and I now is simply a sign of our evolution as a planet and a species.

I don't claim to understand all their abilities. I simply scribe the information I am given, but I have learned a lot about what they can do for us as I work with them daily.

From what I have discovered there are approximately 52,000 archangels, so the few I have named here barely scratches the surface. I have not yet learned how many angels there are.

I am told there are 32 universes, including this one, and archangels can transcend them all, whereas angels cannot. Archangels are omnipresent, meaning they can be in multiple places at once. Angels are not omnipresent.

I am now going to share with you the limited information I have gleaned thus far. I wish it were more and maybe one day it will be.

Archangels:

Archangel Razial
(Masculine energy)
Primary ability is 'psychological health.' Secondary ability is 'Akashic Records,' 'Higher-Self-development,' and 'energetic (being) health.'
*Razial has never incarnated before. He has only ever been an archangel.

Archangel Michael
(Masculine energy)
Primary ability is to 'establish and restore healthy tethers.' Secondary ability is 'detaching unhealthy tethers' and to 'cultivate inspiration.'
*Most humans I have met refer to tethers as cords, but Michael says tethers are the more accurate term.

Archangel Gabriel
(Masculine energy)
Primary ability is 'transport signal related to portals.' Secondary ability is to 'travel through time.'
*Even though time does not really exist. Figure that one out!
*Archangel Gabriel switched to a more feminine energy once to complete a specific task, which intrigued me because I did not know they could do that.

Archangel Tushit
(Masculine energy)
Primary ability is that of a 'master surgeon.'
*Archangel Tushit is the archangel surgeon that helped me with my scoliosis. I just did not know his name at the time.

Archangel Rageal
(Masculine energy)
Primary ability is to 'maximize health. Secondary ability is the 'activation of energetic ability' and 'telepathic communication.'

Archangel Arkapa
(Masculine energy)
Primary ability is 'soul healing.' Secondary ability is 'channeling source energy.'

Archangel Metatron
(Masculine energy)
Primary ability is 'multidimensional evolution.' Secondary ability is 'trans-dimensional geometry.'
*I did ask him once if he really did incarnate as a human before, and he said yes, he had.

Archangel Azrael
(Masculine energy)
Primary ability is 'tapping into realities.' Secondary ability is 'quantum bursts.'

Archangel Pdushf (Which is why I just call him the symbols archangel)
(Masculine energy)
Primary ability is 'symbols,' such as crop circles and those used in attunements.
* Archangel Pdushf is the one that does most of my activations and attunements.

Lord of the Akashic Records
(Masculine energy)
Primary ability is the 'Akashic Records for individuals and universally. All scribing and changes.'
*I asked what his real name was and his reply was, "It's Lord of the Akashic Records."

Archangel Zudkele
(Masculine energy)
Primary ability is 'Multi Frequency projection.'

Archangel Rafiel
(Masculine energy)
Primary ability is the '"I AM" expression.' Secondary ability is 'telekinesis.

Archangel Ecodsif (sounds like echo-d-sif)
(Masculine energy)
Primary ability is to 'work with planets to become healthier.' Secondary ability is 'grounding.'

Archangel Teke (sounds like Tiki)
(Feminine energy)
Primary ability is 'healing and overall health.'

Archangel Ptuk
(Feminine Energy)
Primary ability to assist writers.
* Archangel Ptuk is the one who is helping me to write this book. I am grateful for her help and support.

Archangel Edeny
(Feminine energy)
Primary ability is healing the 'spiritual being.'

Archangel Nepum
(Feminine energy)
Primary ability is helping with 'unforgiveness.' Secondary ability is 'spiritual adaptation.

Archangel Tatum
(Feminine energy)
Primary Ability is 'consoling.'

Angels:

Angel Riddel
(Masculine energy)
Two primary abilities. One is 'keeper of the Akashic Records,' and two is 'spiritual expansion.' Secondary ability is 'spiritual transitions.'

Angel Bezik
(Masculine energy)
Primary ability is 'Akashic Records healing.' Secondary ability is 'shifting into possibilities' (can determine all possible outcomes).

Angel Merillia
(Feminine energy)
Primary ability is maximizing 'emotional health.' Secondary ability is 'maximizing intuitive health.'
*Angel Merillia is 99.9 percent of the Light and the closest angel I know to becoming an archangel.

Angel Ntwoyn
(Feminine energy)
Primary ability is 'hexes and curses.'
*When a friend of mine was hit with a curse from someone in Africa, it was Angel Ntwoyn that helped me nullify and transmute it safely.

Angel Cedual (sounds like Se-dual)
(Masculine energy)
Primary ability is 'ALL chakras and auric field.'
*For the longest time, I referred to him as the Chakra Angel

Angel Lodum
(Feminine energy)
Primary ability is to 'radiate Light.' Secondary ability is to 'maximize clairvoyant health.'

Angel Edley (Sounds like Eedley)
(Feminine energy)
Primary ability is 'links.'

Angel Esh (Sounds like Eesh)
(Feminine energy)
Primary ability is 'Soul retrieval.' Secondary ability is 'dimensional shifts.'

These descriptions tell you what they can do and how they can help us, but do nothing to describe their personalities, which are varied and unique. Each is special in their own way.

My dear Archangel Razial has never incarnated before. He has only ever been an archangel, which I believe is why he is so literal. If I were to describe his energy I would say he was the studious type, with eye glasses to further humanize him.

In bed one evening, Ken and I were reading books but I had become quietly distracted when I became aware of Razial's presence. I was letting him know how grateful I was for him and he was returning the feeling of being grateful for me as well. During this quiet, internal exchange, I noticed Ken sniffling and grabbing a tissue.

"What's wrong?" I asked.

"I don't know," Ken responded, "suddenly, I just feel so happy and grateful for everything I have. I'm so fortunate to have you, the kids, and this house," he said, sniffling with tears of joy.

I hooted with laughter. I knew what had happened because it had happened to me before. When archangels express their emotions towards a human, they tend to swamp us with emotion. Ken had just been caught in the crossfire of Razial expressing his feelings for me. Immediately, Ken asked Razial if that's what had happened and Razial confirmed it.

"I wondered what was going on. One minute I was fine, the next minute I felt overwhelmed with gratitude. I didn't know what for, so I started listing all the things I was grateful for," Ken said, as the understanding dawned on him.

I know archangels have a sense of humor.

I was at a friend's house, because she asked me to do some Akashic Records clearing for her. I never do this without The Lord of the Akashic Records, of course. With his help, we could identify what needed to be cleared. The Lord of the Akashic Records would identify everything and I would transmute it. When I do this, sometimes I get visuals, and sometimes I don't. This time I did. He showed me a huge junk pile and a couch. He was putting more emphasis on the couch, indicating, "Everything and the couch." Huh?

"Oh! Do you mean, everything and the kitchen sink?" I asked him. I felt him smile, proud of his joke, and I howled with laughter. I have no clue if he got the saying wrong intentionally or not, but either way, I thought it was funny.

The next day, I was at my friend's store and in the back office she has a couch. I never noticed the pattern on it before but it was the **exact same couch** that The Lord of the Akashic Records had shown me.

The funniest archangel is Archangel Gabriel. While Ken and I were working with a client, there was a pause in everyone's conversation as we assessed what to do next. In these one-on-one sessions, the client lies on a Reiki bed while I stand over them typically doing energy work, while Ken sits in a chair nearby and channels any directions or information I may need to know as I work. At the beginning of a session I invite in the archangels to help me, and anyone else that would be in the highest and greatest good of the client. As you can imagine, the room gets quite crowded sometimes. When there is silence an angel or archangel sometimes takes the opportunity to tell us something.

Have you ever heard the song by (Rockwell, 1984) called, "Somebody's watching me?" It's the song you hear played most frequently at Halloween.

There was a silence between the three of us and all I heard in my head was to the words to this song being sung, *"Ever feel like, somebody's watching **you**."*

Naturally, I guffawed! Someone had totally changed the words to make it funny. I was too busy laughing to figure out who it was but I told my client and Ken what had happened and Ken figured out it was Archangel Gabriel.

Less funny and more surprising was Archangel Michael. I have always found Michael to be more serious than the others. Stoic is the word I would use.

One evening, Ken and I were sitting across from each doing spiritual work and talking. I was looking him in the eyes, I saw something that stunned me to my core. Unbeknownst to Ken, the sudden appearance of Michael looking back at me through Ken's right pupil shocked me to silence. He observed me as I observed him and no other exchange was made. This only lasted maybe thirty seconds, then as quickly as he appeared, he was gone.

Ken had already given permission to the archangels to work through him so this was not against his will in anyway. Ken was completely unaware of the entire exchange. I never reacted outwardly, so as not to startle Ken. Inside however, I was trying to understand what had just happened. Within minutes I told Ken about the exchange and he was stunned at how he was none the wiser. Then we asked Michael what was the purpose of what he just did? His reply was simple. He simply wanted to see what I looked like through human eyes.

Like most people, I had the perception that angels were perfect in every way and they needed nothing. Well, to me they are perfect in every way, however, I was wrong about them needing nothing.

I was struggling one night, as Ken and I were doing healing work on ourselves. It was around unforgiveness specifically related to one of my past lives. Like a film reel in my mind, I saw the entire event unfold before me.

I was a man in that lifetime. A large man, very muscular, dressed almost like a gladiator I had seen in movies. I wore very little; the waist covering was leather and there was a belt of some sort that held a long sword. I wore a shirt that was open most of the way. I was obviously well known because I saw myself walk through a market of vendors outdoors who greeted me in a friendly manner as I passed.

I spotted a young boy who was being harassed by three grown men. No one else appeared to be willing to intervene. I walked up to them without being noticed and quietly raised my sword to the throat of one of the men, which quickly got their attention and everyone went quiet. I do not remember the conversation word for word but I told them to leave the boy alone or they would have to deal with me. I appeared to be significantly larger than the other men so I assume this was reason enough for them not to argue. Later that night the boy was found murdered.

I was informed that I carried a great deal of unforgiveness for myself in the present, and those men in the past life. Naturally, I tried to forgive them and myself. I said the words and I tried hard to mean them, but it did not clear, which frustrated me.

It was then that Angel Beziq offered to share a similar experience he had as a way of comforting me, I suspect. Through Ken and I, Angel Beziq relayed this series of events.

Before Beziq was an angel he had incarnated once. I do not know for sure whether he incarnated on Earth or another planet but the landscape looked a lot like Earth to me. The scene started with Beziq being chased by one man until he was cornered on a cliffside. Standing very close to the edge, either Beziq lost his balance or the ground gave way and he fell. But he didn't fall to his death. Instead, he landed on an outcropping ledge somewhere below. The man who had been chasing him could see him from above, but instead of helping Beziq, he simply walked away. Beziq yelled and screamed for help until he barely had a voice left. Someone heard him eventually, a few days later, when Beziq was weak, tired, and probably dehydrated. They had tried to help him by lowering various things for Beziq to grab onto so they could pull him up. However, in his weakened state, he was unable to, and he died there on that ledge.

I asked Angel Beziq if he ever forgave the man and he told me he had not. I thought the man who did this would be sorry now. I asked Archangel Razial to find the man who did this to Beziq and ask him if he was sorry. Razial returned with bad news. The man who contributed to Beziq's death was still not sorry. I asked Beziq if he could forgive the man anyway. He said he would try and then left. I felt terrible and asked Angel Merillia if she would comfort Beziq for me and see if she could convince him to forgive the man and himself, and I would do the same with what happened to me.

I knew in my heart I did not want to carry old hurts with me, like Beziq had. It was in that moment that I was able to forgive. I owe that to Beziq. A few days later, I asked Beziq if he had been able to do the same. I was happy to hear he had.

Thank you, Angel Beziq, for teaching me how to forgive and why it's so important.

CHAPTER 14

Symbols

As I am sure you may have noticed on the front cover of book one, *Waking Up An Empath*, and on this book too, there are a number of symbols displayed. One is clearly the Empath symbol as discussed in book one. What you may not know is that there were thirteen symbols on the cover. Some of them were buried into the title of exploding Light. It's now time for me to share all thirteen symbols with you and their meaning.

When you hold your hand over the empath symbol especially, you will probably notice heat on your hand, a tingling sensation, or you may even feel lightheaded. That's because you are connecting with the energy. As of July 2017, the other symbols have not been "activated" or they have not been connected to that energy yet. They will be, soon, when we are ready for it. In the meantime, the Symbols Archangel asked me to make these symbols available, so the people who need them will have them available when the time is right.

In the meantime, we have been trying to learn all we can about the Empath symbol. We discovered that when we put the Empath symbol on various products, the energy the symbol is connected to imbues the person or product with that energy, thereby raising its vibration significantly.

We tested the Empath symbol over and over by having people close their eyes and hold out their hand palm down, and then we would put the symbol from my first book open, under their hand without touching them, and ask them what they felt. Most people said heat, some said tingling, and a few felt lightheaded or dizzy. One person nearly fainted from a standing position so we realized we had to be more careful about testing it out that way.

I decided to tattoo the Empath symbol onto my wrist and tested it that way as well. I asked Ken to hold his hand over my wrist that did not have the tattoo and hold his other hand over my wrist that did have the tattoo to see if he could still feel it. He did. I placed it strategically on my wrist, in the hopes it would help clients as I did energy work on them. It does. Some of my students have done the same by getting it tattooed on themselves as well.

That's when I realized I needed to use this Empath symbol as much as possible, so I had it trademarked to myself and started putting it on everything I could afford. A local glassmaker agreed to make glass pendants that could be worn around people's necks. They are beautiful pieces of handmade work that are sold locally. I also turned the Empath symbol into my brand and started placing it on all products lines I offer, such as my Energy Protection Blend (discussed in chapter 21), other essential oils, glass pendant necklaces, and more to come.

Even though it is trademarked to me, I still encourage people to use it for personal use (no monetary gain). For example, draw it on all your medication bottles, labels of clothing or anywhere else you can think of.

As these new symbols become activated, I will certainly share their various uses as well, probably through my blog at KimWuirch.com.

Synchronism   Awaken   Vibration   Source   Gaia

Archangel   Divine Love   Divinity   Relinquish   Angel

Pure White   Destination   Empath

CHAPTER 15

Two Portals

When Ken was reading my first book, *Waking Up An Empath*, he came to the chapter called Spirit Fair. In that chapter, I talk about the reading Teza did for me. That was the first reading I had ever received from a psychic. She wrote everything down but naturally very little of it made sense to me at the time. It's funny when I look back on it now and realize she wrote down "Archangel Raziel." Funny because she spelled his name wrong too! I had no idea who he was then and his relation to me. Not until later.

On page three of her notes she wrote:

2 Portals

1. *Forgiveness*
2. *Release*

In all Timelines, Dimensions, and Realities

She did not try to explain it and I did not ask. I only learned what it meant 13 months later when Ken read that chapter. My guides told Ken first, as they knew when everything came to light it would rock my world.

Ken was told that I needed to remember the other portal. The first portal was Stonehenge, which I talked about earlier. When he told me, there was another portal, the blood drained from my face. I dreaded another regression but I was urged into it. Against my better judgement, I allowed myself to go into another past life regression session with Ken.

It was 1500 years ago and I was on a beach. I knew it was a beach because I was standing on sand and there was an ocean behind me. I was the observer, watching from afar, seeing myself as a man, with my back to the ocean as I watched some children play. I had an amused expression on my face. I was wearing a tunic with what appeared to be chain mail overtop. A long sword in a hilt was nestled at my hip, one hand resting on it casually. Everything about me seemed plain and average. The wind blew through my light brown hair as I stood there.

From my view as an observer I could see approximately eleven men clearly sneaking past me. Their behavior seemed sly and sneaky as they kept peering over at me. Then I lost sight of them as they got closer to the ocean. I think some time passed as the light seemed to change. Then all hell broke loose.

There was yelling and noise but I don't know why. I saw myself break into a run towards where the men had gone. As I ran I was no longer the observer and I suddenly became one with the man I was then. Fear was coursing through me. I saw the men standing near the shore, not moving, as if they were too shocked. I screamed at them, "YOU FOOLS! YOU STUPID FOOLS, WHAT HAVE YOU DONE?!" I was beyond angry. I saw red. Then I saw nothing but blackness. When the blackness cleared, I knew what I had done.

All of them were dead. Massacred like lambs to the slaughter. They never stood a chance against me.

I dropped to my knees in the wet sand and said, "Gaia, I'm so sorry. I should have protected you."

The men had attempted to alter the portal. Due to their lack of experience and understanding they had made a mistake, causing a massive tear in this realm and several others. The tear hurt Gaia so much. I felt her pain and suffering, and had lashed out at the men for their mistake. For me, it was the equivalent of watching my own child be tortured in front of me. What I now understand is that the men were manipulated by another man. They followed the directions provided by someone who remained hidden.

I do not know what became of me after that but I am aware of the guilt that set in almost immediately.

In the present I came to my present awareness, gagging and heaving, disgusted and horrified by what I had seen and done. Tormented that Gaia (Earth) has suffered every day since. Sobs wracked my body and I gulped for air.

"Gaia, I promise I'll do everything I can to find a way to fix this," I said solemnly.

"Please hurry," Gaia replied.

It was not until the next day that I could fully relay all the details to Ken. Even then I could not speak of it without crying. The healing may have begun, but I had a long way to go yet.

"So, you were the guardian of not one, but two portals that we know of?" Ken asked rhetorically.

"Yes, I suppose so. Razial would know better than I. Ask him, you have my permission," I responded.

"Your guide is an archangel. Two other archangels and angels always seem to be around you," Ken said, knowing the answer once again.

"Obviously. You know that. You talk to Razial and the rest of them all the time," I replied, rolling my eyes.

"Who are you?" Ken asked.

"Don't be silly, you know who I am," I said matter of factly.

"No seriously. Who the F@#% are you?" Ken asked again.

"I am who I've always been, though I've gone by many names. Now knock it off, you're being ridiculous."

CHAPTER 16

Bedtime

It seems the spirit realm has no concept of time. I mean, I understand they know we use time here to manage our lives, but sometimes I think they forget or they don't care. Either way, I get cranky when I am awoken from a deep sleep.

To my dismay, spirit continues to wake me up at all hours of the night.

Even while I am sleeping, I am very aware of who or what is around me. One night I woke up to an old man standing at the end of my bed staring at me. He scared the crap out of me and I screamed the house down. I was sure the protection I had placed on the house would work, but it doesn't work when they attach themselves to living things (like my dog). Sneaky! Ken was wide awake at this point anyway, so I banished the soul from my room and asked the angel who helps souls cross over to please see if she could help him cross so I could go back to sleep.

Another time I felt a presence beside me on my side of the bed. I had my back turned to that side of the bed and in my barely awake state I ninja jumped over Ken to the complete opposite side of the bed as I screamed. It turns out it was a new angel I had not met before, so I was unfamiliar with her energy. I scared her as much as she scared me! I tried to coax her back, to no avail. The next day I found out what the message was, only after I got Razial to tell her I was sorry and I didn't mean to spaz out like that.

One time I was not awakened during the night. Instead I woke up in the morning to my touch lamp being turned on. Both Ken and I were puzzled as to why. I woke up in the middle of the king-size bed, furthest away from the lamp, and in all the years I have had it, it has never turned on of its own accord. Upon further investigation, we discovered it was an angel who wanted to see if she could manipulate the electricity to turn the lamp on. Well, bravo! You succeeded. It works during the day too. Just saying. But I can't complain, as at least she didn't wake me up.

I know I communicate with both archangels and angels while I sleep, but to this day I still have difficulty remembering the details. To help me with this they have a clever way of making sure I wake up to a known song in my head. I hear the lyrics and music playing in my mind. I quite enjoy waking up to a song and wish they would make this happen more often. When I awaken this way, I know some part of the song has a message for me, and all I need to do is get the full lyrics to the song, so I can pinpoint the message. Waking up to a song does put me in a better mood about being awake.

CHAPTER 17

Spirit Expos

Ken and I attend many public spirit expos and spiritual events where I work as a healer and sign books. I also teach a lot of two-day workshops such as Usui Reiki, Akashic Records, and two-hour workshops, such as empath development, as well as various other fun workshops. No two events are ever the same. We have had some interesting experiences at some of them. I'll share a few with you.

As most events, I advertise that I do Chakra Clearing. It comes across as non-threatening. Most people know what chakras are, plus they are usually aware that having them working in balance is ideal. Of course, once they sit down and I assess them, I use every modality I have at my disposal to help them in that twenty short minutes.

One gentleman sat down in my chair and I asked if he was looking for anything specific. "No, not really," he said, in a voice so quiet I could barely hear him. I worked on him without touching him at all. I used only my spiritual abilities to clear his throat chakra where I could feel that something significant had happened. I asked him a few questions until I learned he had died, and ever since he had been resuscitated his voice had never returned to full volume.

From what I could figure out, this happened as he was transitioning back into his body. I continued to work until the end of our twenty minutes, and we remained in silence until we were done. When I asked how he felt I was stunned by the change in his voice! He was speaking clearly and at a volume I could hear! Even he noticed right away and called his daughter over. She could not believe the sudden change in his voice either. He was relieved, because he said people were constantly asking him to speak up, but he couldn't. It was frustrating for him and I could understand why. I watched him regain so much confidence in that moment and it was a good reminder of why I do this work.

At a completely different event I was working on a gentleman, whom I assumed from his appearance had a native heritage. I started scanning him with my hands like I always do with clients. With my hands about six inches away from his body I quickly felt for areas of disruption, temperature changes, and the various other sensations that indicate where I need to focus. However, as I scanned him I felt nothing, which left me feeling momentarily confused. This rarely happens to me but now and again I may need to ask the individual for permission to do energy work on them. I asked the gentleman for permission, which he gave, and I proceeded to scan him again. On the second attempt, everything was as I expected and I identified what I needed to work on.

The energy work was simple and I completed this rapidly. For the second part, however, I was stumped. It was clear to me that I needed to help him do something but I did not know what. I asked Ken to assist me, as I sometimes do. To help me, I asked him to tune in and see if he could get more detail on what I needed to do next. I said the energy work was complete but there was some other way I could help this client.

Ken agreed, and sat down to close his eyes and focus. He started to relay the information that was coming through, but it felt 'off' to me. Something was not right. I didn't say anything as I pondered this. Then Ken exclaimed, "I don't know what just happened… I lost all spiritual connection! I can't talk to anyone or get anything now." He did not sound at all pleased.

"Drat!" I said. "Okay, don't panic. I'll figure it out. I'm just going to have to try harder to focus." I sat down and closed my eyes. Instantly, in my mind, I saw a tall native man with a full feather headdress. He did not smile, he did not speak, and his arms were crossed across his chest. He was a chief. I asked if he was there to protect my client and I got a single and abrupt nod as a response. I asked him if he blocked my partner because he did not have permission to access my client. Another single, abrupt nod. Then he showed me that he basically flicked Ken's third eye and shut him down.

I asked the native chief he could be clearer about what else my client required of me. He showed me an image of my client in a meditative state as he reached out to his guides. I then understood what he wanted me to do and I thanked him. I thanked him again for allowing me to do spiritual work on what was clearly land he protected as well. With a curt nod, he left.

Well, that was interesting.

I turned back to my client and told him he had a very powerful chief watching over him and the protection was strong. I told him how lucky he was because I had yet to come across someone who was shielded the way he was. I explained to him that this chief wanted him to contact them more often. Through touch I took him up to a higher plain of existence, so he would know what it felt like when he tried to do it on his own.

After my client had gone, I explained to Ken what had happened. "They can do that?!" Ken asked.

"Apparently, they can. I suggest if you know you're on native land or what may have been considered sacred land that could still be protected, check in and see if anyone objects to you doing spiritual work," I said, laughing.

Within a few minutes, I re-established Ken's spiritual abilities and he was back in action but I could tell he was not very happy that the "non-living" knew how to shut him down. I think I heard him muttering something about figuring out his own protection so they could not violate him like that again. I did my best not to laugh as I turned away.

We were at a spirit expo and Ken and I attended a past life regression workshop for fun.

There were about thirty chairs all facing a stage, so Ken and I found seats together in the middle, about six rows back from the front. The man leading the workshop spoke into a microphone so we could all hear his instructions. He recited a relaxing meditation and slowly directed us into our past lives. Soon I stopped hearing what he was saying as I became immersed in the memory.

It was a small house, quite narrow and simple. From the front door, there was a narrow and steep wooden staircase that went up to a second floor. On the main floor was a small living room and the kitchen was in the back. I was a woman in this lifetime, middle-age, between thirty and thirty-five. My dark hair was pulled back in a bun and I wore a plain dress. I was in the kitchen when my husband came in drunk, which seemed to anger me. I was clearly instigating an argument, and when my husband went upstairs I followed, still badgering him about something. I don't know exactly what we were arguing about, but at the top of the stairs he turned suddenly and shoved me. I ended up at the bottom of the stairs with a broken neck. Dead instantly.

In the present, I got a bad case of the giggles. I had seen myself die so many times that it no longer fazed me. My giggling got Ken's attention, so I whispered to him what happened when everyone else in the group was sharing. "Guess how I died this time!" I said to Ken, and then I told him the story. Finally, I calmed down and got ahold of myself.

We were starting the next round, except this time we were directed to go to a time in a future life. I closed my eyes preparing to follow the directions provided. We were instructed to imagine ourselves at the top of a marble staircase.

Well that was it, I could not help it! I slapped my hands over my mouth and laughed into my hands as tears of mirth rolled down my face. "Not another staircase! And a hard marble one no less!" I whispered to Ken, who was laughing too. We were starting to draw the attention of the other attendees. "What is it with me and staircases?" I asked Ken.

CHAPTER 18

Auralite-23

My friend Liane works with a very special crystal called Auralite23, which looks at a lot like Amethyst. We both feel that the world needs to be made aware of this very special crystal and its properties for healing. For that reason, she wrote a chapter for me to include and share with my readers.

I still remember the first time I worked with this crystal. Liane has a large and heavy Auralite23 crystal, which she lovingly calls Max, that she allows people to hold and receive its healing benefits. I had been experiencing chest pains in the center of my chest... nothing serious but enough to be annoying. Archangel Razial nudged me to get Liane to take a picture of my auric field to see what was going on. I had never expressed interest in aura photography before but it seemed important at the time and I knew Liane's Kirilian photography equipment was legit, so I agreed. I called her up and told her I needed my aura mapped out and asked her how soon could she do it. Funnily enough she could do it immediately, but she would not be able to print off the results because her printer was not working. I was fine with that, so I went to her store.

The results shocked us both.

When the scanning was complete the computer generated an image on the screen. My chakras were all in perfect balance and health, which I expected. However, what I did not expect was to see, was the shape of a perfect 5-point quartz crystal, pointed at either end right in the middle of my chest.

The reason, we were told, is that in previous lifetimes, we did not have the ability to draw in a significant amount of source energy into our bodies to channel energy for various spiritual purposes. Somehow, I had created this "battery pack" within me a long time ago. By having it there, it had allowed me to heal others and use spiritual abilities that most others could not. No wonder I had been called a witch, a shaman, and a druid, among other labels applied to me over my lifetimes.

I no longer needed it, I was informed. It was detrimental now, because in this lifetime I could freely draw on source energy, and having this battery within me was causing me to carry too much energy in my body. So, it was then that Liane handed me "Max." After 15 minutes holding the Auralite23 crystal, Liane rescanned my entire auric field. The shape of the 5-point crystal had gone and I didn't even have a printout to prove it was there in the first place.

I hope you enjoy learning about Auralite23!

The Unveiling of a Crystal – When Humanity Needs It the Most

Written by Liane Pinel (Pinel, 2017) - Crystal Healer, Intuitive Counselor, Witch, and owner of The Spirit Within Metaphysical Store and Event Centre.

Photo provided by Liane Pinel

Auralite-23 is a crystal of pure nature that has never been experienced anywhere else on Earth. In addition to the minerals that compose amethyst, scientists have identified the presence of 23 other elements and minerals, hence the name Auralite-23. Together these components create the most powerful crystal known to man thus far. This crystal is literally more than 23 crystals in ONE! It comes out of the earth already activated and it never needs cleansing. It cleanses and recharges other crystals it encounters. More importantly, it is a crystal that is here to help awaken humanity!

In general, human beings have this thing about needing to know "what" something is before placing value on it, so I will give you the science behind it, as I know it.

This unique Crystalline Entity has come from The Sacred Cave of Wonders (located within the Boreal Forest of the Canadian Shield, 800 km north of Thunder Bay, Ontario) where the most unique crystals on earth have been created from the "bones of Mother Earth."

Auralite-23 is also called Red Cap Amethyst, Auralite Amethyst, Kindred Spirit, or Super 23. Auralite-23 is the name of a new discovery of an ancient field of amethyst crystals that formed in the very apex of the mysterious Keweenawan Rift between 1.1 and 1.5 billion years ago during the Mesoproterozoic era of the Precambrian.

When the Mid-continent Rift System tried, and failed to tear the North American continent apart, 23 elements and minerals filled in the gap left behind. No continent has ever survived a catastrophic event like this, and never has one healed itself! No known rift system has ever failed to become an ocean. Auralite-23 is in the center of one of the greatest mysteries in geological history. Therefore, Auralite-23 is the most significant crystalline discovery of our time.

Auralite-23 has been scientifically proven as one of the world's oldest crystal gemstones, which developed and grew more than 1.1 billion years ago while the first signs of life appeared on Earth. Each element and mineral that makes up the Auralite-23 crystal reflects its own journey frozen in time.

Here are the many benefits of Auralite-23:

It connects to your guardian like a twin spirit. This crystal reminds us of how we are alike, that "All is One." It reads into the individual's spirit, searching and highlighting what needs to be cleared. Due to this crystal's relaxing and spiritual properties, it can be very supportive during meditation, astral travel, and past life regression.

Auralite-23 helps to remove the feelings of burden and stress. It envelopes the being with an air of calm and brings gentle waves of soothing energy. Where there are low emotions and depression, Auralite-23 can help to lift away those energies.

Auralite-23 helps to ease anxiety, nerves, and the intensity of panic attacks. It can be held during times of shock and distress. This is a crystal that can help ease, and even put a stop, to sleep disorders that are related to insomnia. It can help remove prejudice and find our inner voice again. It reminds the body of its proper vital functions and aids in cellular regeneration.

Auralite-23 resonates well with the body's energy centers, especially from the heart center, up to the crown center. It is a crystal that removes and wards away negativity, replacing it with positivity. Auralite-23 helps us to love and be loved, to find peace within our hearts, and, to be happy. It wakes us up to our universal energy, which connects us to every other human on this planet.

Here is a summary of the components present in Auralite-23:

Amethyst

Associated with the Crown and Third Eye Chakras, Amethyst has a very powerful spiritual vibration. It protects against negative vibrations, including psychic attacks, transforming them into loving energy. Amethyst seals holes in the aura, purifying and protecting it. It harmonizes the physical body with its healing field. Amethyst is one of the best crystals to stimulate the Third Eye and enable out of body experiences. It brings stability, strength, inspiration, and it helps us to make good decisions. It also assists in meditation and deepens concentration.

Titanite

By activating the Solar Plexus, Titanite releases a strong feeling of joy. It also stimulates the three lower chakras simultaneously. Titanite inspires enthusiasm, quick thinking, courage, and stimulates the libido.

Cacoxenite (also known as The Melody Stone or Super Seven – containing seven minerals in its make up)

It helps develop psychic abilities, because it strengthens the presence of cosmic energies in the upper chakras. It also stimulates cell regeneration.

Lepidocrocite

The high vibrations of Lepidocrocite opens the crown chakra to the Divine. The energy flows to the heart and expands all higher chakras, dissolving negative energies.

Ajoite

Ajoite releases feelings of anger, resentment, and pain. It helps to feel compassion for oneself as well as for others. It is a very nurturing stone, Ajoite heals the healer. It activates the Heart and Throat Chakras and enables us to communicate from the heart. It heals, strengthens, and harmonizes the emotional body. It awakens the heart to the imaginative realms.

Hematite

Hematite is useful to create peaceful and loving relationships. It calms the mind and leads us to self-knowledge. Hematite is associated with courage, self-confidence, stability, and personal magnetism. Mostly associated with the base chakras, it also helps to balance all the chakras.

Magnetite

Magnetite is associated with the Root Chakra, but it aligns all chakras and meridians with the subtle bodies. It calms meridians that have too much energy and activates those that need more. It helps with convalescence after illness. It enables telepathy and attracts love, loyalty, and abundance. It reduces negative emotions and attracts positive feelings.

Pyrite

Associated with the Solar Plexus, Third Eye, and Root Chakras, Pyrite brings joy and abundance. It helps with making good business decisions and attracts prosperity. Pyrite can counteract chronic fatigue and help with memory and creativity. It enhances psychic abilities and brings a strong protection to the physical and subtle bodies. Pyrite may be used to bring positive vibrations into a room or office.

Goethite

Goethite is a stone that encourages a deep connection with the Earth. It is a discovery stone, and brings awareness to a Soul's plan. It awakens compassion and love and is used by counsellors to assist in getting in touch with one's repressed grief to begin healing emotionally. It opens the way to understanding of love, joy, pain, and grief.

Pyrolusite

Pyrolusite is very useful in clearing the environment of negative energy and dispelling psychic attacks. It can clear the intentions of those who inhabit the lower frequencies of the Astral World. Pyrolusite blocks negative mental influences, and releases energy blockages caused by harmful thoughts. It is a stone of optimism, material comfort, and intellect.

Gold

Gold is a protective and purifying metal, and for millennia it has been believed to help with stabilizing, harmonizing, and grounding the body. Gold is a symbol of prosperity, success, love, and illumination. It can be used to activate the Solar Plexus and the Crown Chakras. It inspires a sense of morality, integrity, and purity of the mind.

Silver

Silver has a soothing and calm energy. It is a powerful metal that enhances intuition, love, and protection.

Platinum

Platinum is the metal for wisdom. It is an excellent element to use for deep meditation. It helps us to discover our true mission in life.

Nickel

Nickel extends into many dimensions. It is useful when additional information or energy is required, thereby advancing knowledge to help with personal breakthroughs.

Copper

Being a conductive mineral, it neutralizes problems caused by electromagnetic fields. Copper helps to perceive energy at different levels, including cosmic energy. It also enhances consciousness.

Iron

Iron works as well at the Earth level as it does at the cosmic level. You can use iron as a grounding tool for earthly work, and at the same time, as a universal tool for spiritual development. Iron is a good material for out of body experiences and shamanic travel.

Limonite

A grounding stone, Limonite stimulates inner strength. It provides protection to the physical body during metaphysical activities, and it defends against mental influence and psychic attacks. Limonite also allows us to stand firm without needing to fight back.

Sphalerite

Sphalerite raises our frequency. It allows the development of extra-sensorial gifts. Sphalerite brings us energy and improves the nervous system.

Covellite

Covellite is associated with the Root, Third Eye, and Crown chakras. Covellite is a stone of transition and it helps to heal deep wounds. It also helps to achieve higher vibration levels. It accelerates our spiritual development by increasing our intuition and psychic abilities.

Chalcopyrite

Chalcopyrite activates and purifies all the chakras. It helps us be flexible, open us up to new paradigms, and brings a feeling of joy. It helps our perceptions follow good energy transitioning us towards a more positive attitude.

Epidote

Epidote is a stone that enhances emotional and spiritual growth. It cleanses emotional scars and helps to eliminate them permanently. It brings hope. It repels close mindedness and negative criticism. Epidote enables spiritual growth and enhances perceptions. It is an excellent stone for empowering one to participate in all levels of life.

Gialite

Gialite is associated with the Root Chakra and is an excellent grounding stone. It controls negative energy by keeping it at bay.

Bornite

Bornite transmutes negative beliefs making it easier to deal with difficult situations. Bornite reduces the mundane and superficial to clear the way for spiritual growth.

Rutile

A powerful healing and protection stone, Rutile is associated with all chakras. It pierces through the density of the physical, emotional, and mental bodies. It protects the physical body and the subtle bodies. It develops strength in each person and slows down the aging process. It increases positive energy and can enhance relationships. Rutile increases the potential for clairvoyance.

That is the science, energy, and metaphysical musings that have been discovered about Auralite-23 for many years. It changed my life and that of my clients for the better... so much better. I teach about it across Canada and I am planning to write a book about it with loads more experiential teachings and explanations. Why? Because I KNOW it CAN and HAS and WILL continue to change lives. In the first six months of working with "Max" I purchased my own home, was debt free, and most important of all, I felt happy! All I had to do was listen… to a rock!

For more information about Auralite-23, contact Liane Pinel at her store, The Spirit Within.
Email: TheSpiritWithinEventCentre@gmail.com

CHAPTER 19

Is it true?

Just because someone is famous does not mean they are right about everything. I hope by the time you get to the end of this chapter you will understand why I said that, but more importantly why it's true.

There are many spiritual leaders, gurus, enlightened people, those who have 20 years of spiritual experience, and so on. These people tend to be the pioneers of a new way of thinking, a new way of living, and potentially a new way of being. I commend them for their efforts. I congratulate them for going outside of everyone's comfort zone to try something new and show the world there are, in fact, other ways to do things. They deserve respect and consideration no doubt.

Where I have concerns, is when people start to idolize those who become famous. I have concerns when folks take everything as fact if it comes from the lips of a known guru. I can tell when a person puts others on a pedestal and elevates them above themselves because of infamy. There is a very specific energy about it. A vibration that makes the hair on the back of my neck stand on end. It's not healthy at all.

I had to call Ken to task about this. Since I met him, he was almost always quoting facts from someone else. He rarely spoke his own words or thoughts but rather the words of others. "My guru taught me this," he would say or, "I learned this from so and so." I knew this was not a healthy habit but I let it slide, as I knew the day would arrive when it would be the appropriate time to address it.

When that day came, Ken was arguing with me about the accuracy of some spiritual topic. Typically, I would let it go, even if I knew what he was saying was not accurate. Either I knew it would result in an argument or it was simply not the right time. This time was different because it related directly to a client of ours. I refused to allow him to mislead a client. He could believe whatever he wanted, but if he was going to lead others in his way of thinking and it was not accurate, that was not okay with me. I told him, "Sorry but what you're saying is simply not true." "Yes, it is!" he said, defensively.

"No Ken, it's not," I said in return.

"It's true because I learned that from my guru five years ago," he snapped back at me.

"What, so because they're a guru they must be right every time? Or is it because they're famous? Maybe if you stopped idolizing them you might start to think for yourself. You can check with your guides, or with angels or for that matter with my guide. Ask Razial," I said flatly.

"I don't need to. I know it's right," Ken said, still being defensive.

"Well then what are you afraid of? Why can't you confirm that you and your guru are right? Are you worried I might be right and somehow this person you keep idolizing won't be so perfect anymore? Ask Razial. I know for a fact that you're a strong and accurate channeler, so CHECK!" I said.

"FINE!" Ken snapped back.

A quiet minute passed. Ken finally opens his eyes.

"Crap. What I learned wasn't accurate," Ken said in a sulky voice.

"Ken, it's time for you to stand on your own, instead of in everyone else's shadow. You have a powerful ability. I know because I helped you hone it and increase it. I have the ability, the same as you to verify every scrap of information that comes our way. The only difference is, I question everything, even the things I always thought to be true. It's time you do the same."

I know it's not easy to get everything right when it comes to using psychic abilities. I don't expect anyone to be right a hundred percent of the time. Instead, what I am suggesting is to be open to verifying what you are told and what you have always believed.

Someone may share something with you and you may say, "Nope that doesn't resonate with me, so I'm going to disregard it completely." I caution you about doing this. Sometimes when things don't resonate with you, it's NOT because the information wasn't accurate. It might be because your filters are clogged with old belief systems, emotional baggage, or lower energy.

Instead, I recommend that you listen and be open to another possibility. If it doesn't resonate with you then leave it for now. But be open to the possibility that it might become true for you later. Leave the door open instead of slamming the door shut and refusing to consider that idea again. Alternatively, you can ask your Higher Self or your guides, "If that's not accurate what is more accurate? What would be true in this case? What are the other options?"

Personally, I have days where everything comes through clearly and easily. There is no doubt what I am getting is accurate and true. Every detail of an image is crisp when using my clairvoyance. The clarity of the words coming from the archangel is as easy as a human conversation when using my clairaudience. The words to the song and the feelings projected with it make it obvious what they are trying to tell me when I use my clairsentience. The associated physical sensations, along with the messages, all click. Those are the days I know to use my abilities to the fullest advantage. I can ask my questions, verify things that have been bothering me, or information I need to know to move forward. These are the days when I receive symbols and formulas. Some days I get advice and guidance. Other days I can ask questions about my background. These are the days I ask, "How can I be of service to humanity?"

Then there are other days when the visions are sporadic. The words seem choppy. The feelings and physical sensations are intermittent. I still try on those days. I do my best to get what I can, but I understand it may not be totally accurate and I will have to recheck it all later.

The worst days are when nothing at all comes through. On such days, I may feel lonely and isolated, as if I have lost my very best friend. In the early days of my awakening, I would often feel depressed on these days. Now I know it will pass. The temporary cut off happens for various reasons but usually because my body is changing on some level, physically or otherwise. Either my abilities are increasing or I am clearing out that which no longer serves me. On those days I occupy myself with my worldly needs and those of my family, leaning on my friends for extra support.

Ken has the same ups and downs as I do, sometimes at the same time. If one of us "disconnected" it is preferable we rely on the other, but when we are both disconnected at the same time we sigh and continue with our day. Occasionally we have had to cancel a client session because neither of us would be able to connect with our guides or the client's guides.

Do you want to know what Ken and I were arguing about?

Ken was convinced that Mercury Retrograde affected humans and that no one should sign contracts during that time.

I told him it's a made-up human notion that when Mercury is in Retrograde affects anyone, spiritually or otherwise. Razial tells me it has no effect on humans whatsoever. What really happens is that people literally collapse their energy fields in on themselves during that time. They disempower themselves based on a belief, which is unfortunate because this causes people to feel unwell or negative.

During the first year of my awakening, I had this belief, and I too, was collapsing my energy field. I was complaining about all the ill effects I was experiencing due to "Mercury Retrograde." Once Razial enlightened me to the truth of the matter I immediately stopped believing I could be affected by Mercury Retrograde, which really meant I stopped collapsing my energy field.

I can honestly say I have not been affected by it since.

CHAPTER 20

Sophisticated Beings

Human beings are sophisticated. There is no denying that. To learn how to help people with their self-healing I needed to learn about the different aspects that make up a human being. Together, Ken and I came up with this list of all the various aspects of a human being, and while there is certainly more, these were the primary ones we needed to focus on.

This list is incomplete and it is a work in progress but this information alone has helped so many people.

13 Primary Aspects of a Human Being:

1. Emotional Being
2. Mental Being
3. Spiritual Being
4. Physical Being
5. Energetic Being
6. Ego
7. Vanity
8. Personality
9. Conscience
10. Soul
11. I AM Being
12. Etheric Self

13. Individual Intuition/Higher Self

The **Emotional Being** includes emotions that scale from the lowest vibrations of fear to the highest vibrations of love. Emotions should never be stored in this part of our being; they should only be generated and emitted.

The **Mental Being** is another well-understood part of our being. It's the logical part of us that rationalizes, calculates, and plans. When people speak of "The Mind," they are referring to a part of the Mental Being.

The **Spiritual Being** connects you to different timelines, dimensions, and realms. It also generates spiritual abilities, such as, clairaudience (psychic hearing), clairsentience (psychic feeling), clairvoyance (psychic seeing), clairgustance (psychic tasting) and clairalience (psychic smelling).

The **Physical Being** is our physical form that we use as a vehicle while we are incarnated. Our physical body can store physical traumas or emotional traumas and the accumulated energy can become a blockage that needs to be cleared. There are the obvious traumas that are caused by accident or intention that hurt, harm or disfigure the body. Less obvious afflictions can be done to the body through harmful foods and other items we ingest. All of them impact the physical being. Affected areas could be organs, glands, or systems of the body.

Energetic Being is the aspect of us that relates specifically to the movement of energy. This includes but is not limited to our chakras and our auric fields. I typically see it as electrical energy. Chi, Paraná, Ki, and Life Force Energy is generated from the energetic being. Leading-edge Kirlian photography can capture the health and state of the Energetic Being.

Ego/Vanity/Personality/Conscience. I listed these separately above but they are more like one aspect of you, because they are all linked and they operate as one. If someone were to slice them like a pie, the ego and personality would be the larger slices, the vanity slightly smaller, and the conscience the smallest of all four. This is how it's meant to be.

However, it's common for any of the four to increase in size, causing one or more of the others to decrease in proportion. When this happens, it's known as being out of balance.

Unfortunately, there is a misconception that the ego is bad and must be removed. This is not true. Why would you be created with something that was not needed? You wouldn't. The ego is there to protect you, but if it is not in balance, it may simply need rebalancing.

When the conscience it out of balance to the point that it is nearly nonexistent, we recognize this as a sociopath on the most extreme end of the scale.

The **Soul** resides around the same place as the solar plexus chakra and carries information and knowledge about you as an individual, and it knows what you came here to achieve. Your soul's primary purpose is to seek that which allows it to evolve.

Neale Donald Walsh said it best in *Conversations with God, Book Four, Awakening of the Species*. "Your soul is the local presence of the Divine Intention, which is to express Divinity in every moment as each sentient being defines it."

The **I AM Being** provides instructions to all other aspects of your being to keep everything working together as one. It acts almost like a supervisor and it is like the spokesperson for the other twelve aspects I listed.

The **Etheric Self** is the white halo that surrounds the body. Some of you may have seen this white halo around an individual, which indicates their overall health. The etheric self seems to be the place where most people's traumas are stored from this life and past lives. Another indicator that someone's health is poor is that white halo will be very close to the body. A wider white halo indicates greater health.

Individual Intuition/Higher Self as already discussed, your Higher Self resides as part of your Etheric Self and holds information about you.

Most of my experience with the different aspects came from helping Ken to heal over the course of an entire year. Most of his greatest challenges came from the fact that the various aspects of his beings were not working together as one and that each was unhealthy in a different way. It was clear how this was affecting his life. As a teenager, he struggled with addictions and depression. As an adult, he struggled with working, proper sleeping habits, low self-esteem, healthy relationships (or lack thereof), anger issues, and other emotional extremes. The list goes on. When I met Ken, he was underweight and miserable but he put on a brave front and kept trying to get the healing he needed. For ten years, he tried everything.

In one year working with me, he's now a completely different person and he worked hard for it. It took a lot of humility, strength, and perseverance to get to where he is now. He never gave up, so I never gave up on him.

CHAPTER 21

Infinity Healing

When Ken and I first started working together, before we started taking clients, we mostly worked on each other. Through much trial and tribulation, endless hours of channeling, and hundreds of questions, we eventually came up with a checklist. This became the starting point we used for every client and for ourselves to determine what needed to be addressed regarding spiritual healing. Every individual was different and unique of course. When something new came up, we would add it to our list, which I will share with you:

- o   Lower Energy
- o   Static, Distortion, and Interference
- o   Curses and Hexes
- o   Psychic Attacks
- o   Hooks and Drains
- o   Contracts, Deals, and Agreements
- o   Imprints
- o   Attachments
- o   Spiritual Parasites
- o   Links
- o   Spiritual Being
- o   Emotional Being
- o   Mental Being

o Energetic Being
o Physical Being
o Traumas
o Transitions
o Unhealthy Beliefs
o Tethers (also known as cords)
o Unforgiveness
o Auric Field and Chakras
o Past Lives
o Soul Retrieval
o Other

Every so often we would have to Google a word and look at every synonym until we found the word the archangels approved of, as the closest match in the human language. We learned that each item on the list cannot be healed or cleared in the same way. Each item had to be managed in a specific manner. That, too, took months to understand how best to address each one. Some require energy work, much like Reiki. Others required Akashic Record changes. A few could be managed by myself. Some I was not spiritually strong enough to deal with yet, so we had to request the assistance of an angel or archangel. Fortunately, as we healed and evolved, we learned that Ken was destined to focus all his energies and training on being the best channeler he could be. I, on the other hand, was to focus on strengthening my energy channeling and healing abilities, through practice, attunements, and activations. Many of these attunements and activations were provided by an archangel because no one else on the planet could pass them to me. Often, these attunements and activations came from the Symbols Archangel. I could feel when he was working on me because it would feel like someone was playing with the fine hairs on the top of my head. It was the lightest, gentlest touch, yet I was fully aware of it. On occasion, his work would give me a mild headache or the top of my head would feel like it was on fire! The feeling always passed quickly though.

I will try to explain the list we created to the best of my ability although my understanding is still far from complete. I was assured I did not need to understand each item fully as the archangels working with us would always identify the needed healing and assist as required. I will also mention my preferred method of spiritual healing modality for clearing each item on the list, and the level of spiritual complexity from low, medium, high, to advanced.

Spiritual Being; Connects you to different timelines and dimensions. It also generates spiritual abilities, such as, clairaudience (psychic hearing), clairsentience (psychic feeling), clairvoyance (psychic seeing), clairgustance (psychic tasting) and clairalience (psychic smelling).

Preferred method: Reiki and Command, "I hereby increase and maximize the spiritual being in all timelines, dimensions, and realities. By my will, so it is."
Spiritual complexity: Low
Angel/Archangel to call upon: Archangel Edeny

Emotional Being; Emotions that scale from the lowest vibrations of fear to the highest vibrations of love. Emotions should never be stored in this part of our being; they should only be generated and emitted.

Preferred method: Reiki and Command, "I hereby increase and maximize the emotional being in all timelines, dimensions, and realities. By my will, so it is."
Spiritual complexity: Low
Angel/Archangel to call upon: Angel Merillia

Mental Being; Is the logical part of us that rationalizes, calculates, and plans. When people speak of "The Mind," they are referring to a part of the Mental Being.

Preferred method: Reiki and Command, "I hereby increase and maximize the mental being in all timelines, dimensions, and realities. By my will, so it is."
Spiritual complexity: Low
Angel/Archangel to call upon: Archangel Razial

Energetic Being; Is the aspect of us that relates specifically to the movement of energy. This includes but is not limited to our chakras and our auric field. I typically see it as electrical energy. Chi, Paraná, Ki, and Life Force Energy that is generated from the energetic being. Leading-edge Kirlian photography can capture the health and state of the Energetic Being.

Preferred method: Reiki and Command, "I hereby increase and maximize the energetic being in all timelines, dimensions, and realities. By my will, so it is."
Spiritual complexity: Low
Angel/Archangel to call upon: Angel Cedual (Chakra Angel)

Lower Energy; Often relates to the energy created from lower vibration emotions, such as anger, hatred, sadness, jealousy, and the like. Generated from the individual and the collective.

Preferred method: Reiki, energy protection oil blend (discussed in chapter 21) or any simple form of spiritual energy clearing of which there are many. This can also be done with the command, "I hereby transmute all lower energy in all timelines, dimensions, and realities. By my will, so it is."
Spiritual Complexity: Low
Angel/Archangel to call upon: Not required

Attachments; Not all attachments are unhealthy. This only applies to unhealthy attachments. For example, the bond between the parent and a young child would be considered a healthy attachment.

An unhealthy attachment can be to any person, place, thing, or circumstance that does not serve ones highest and greatest good.

Preferred method: Command, "I hereby transmute all attachments that are not serving my highest and greatest good. By my will, so it is."
Spiritual complexity: Low
Angel/Archangel to call upon: Not required

Static, Distortion, and Interference; Typically generated from environmental disruptions, either man made (various electronics/signals) or disruptions in space (solar flares, meteor showers, magnetic changes, and so on).

Preferred method: Command, "I hereby transmute all static, distortion, and interference in all timelines, dimensions, and realities. By my will, so it is."
Spiritual Complexity: Low
Angel/Archangel to call upon: Not required

Hooks and Drains; Very small energetic hooks (that looks like fishing hooks with fishing line) that drains the individual of minute amounts of energy. This occurs unintentionally from other individuals.

Preferred method: Command, "I hereby transmute all hooks and drains in all timelines, dimensions, and realities. By my will, so it is."
Spiritual Complexity: Low
Angel/Archangel to call upon: Not required

Physical Being; We use our physical form as a vehicle while we are incarnated. Our physical body can store physical traumas or emotional traumas and the accumulated energy can become a blockage that needs to be cleared. Obvious traumas are caused by accident or intention that hurt, harm or disfigure the body. Less obvious afflictions can be done to the body through harmful foods and other items we ingest. All of them impact the physical being. Affected areas could be organs, glands, or systems of the body.

Preferred method: Reiki and Command, "I hereby increase and maximize the physical being in all timelines, dimensions, and realities. By my will, so it is."
Spiritual complexity: Low → Medium
Angel/Archangel to call upon: Archangel Tushit (Surgeon)

<u>Psychic Attacks</u>; Intentional and unintentional lower vibration feelings directed towards an individual(s). An example is if you accidently cut someone off in traffic and they project ill thoughts and feelings towards you.

Preferred method: Command, "I hereby transmute all psychic attacks in all timelines, dimensions, and realities. By my will, so it is."
Spiritual complexity: Low → Medium
Angel/Archangel to call upon: Ask for the archangel who can assist with psychic attacks (this archangel has no name)

<u>Tethers</u> **(also known as Cords);** Unlike links, tethers are energetic cords between souls or beings that create an energetic connection whereby influence is passed between those individuals.

Preferred method: First, ask Archangel Michael to identify all unhealthy tethers for the individual. Allow at least half an hour for him to identify them, or if you can communicate with him, wait until he says he is done before you make the command. Command, "I hereby unplug and transmute all tethers identified by Archangel Michael, and seal all openings left from unplugging tethers in all timelines, dimensions, and realities. By my will, so it is." Then ask Archangel Michael to transmute any that you may have missed and to seal any openings you may have missed.
Spiritual complexity: Medium
Angel/Archangel to call upon: Archangel Michael

Links; Unlike tethers, links are bonds between souls or beings that create a psychic connection in which information is passed between those individuals. There are no energy cords.

Preferred method: First ask Angel Edley to identify all links for the individual. Command, "I hereby transmute all links identified by Angel Edley, in all timelines, dimensions, and realities. By my will, so it is."
Spiritual complexity: Medium
Angel/Archangel to call upon: Angel Edley

Imprints; These are the impressions left with you, often from those of influence in your life. Like branding livestock, the imprint is impressed upon you and will stick with you through your life and possibly lifetimes. Unlike beliefs, imprints are observed and leave an impression on your psyche.

Preferred method: Command, "I hereby transmute all imprints in all timelines, dimensions, and realities. By my will, so it is."
Spiritual Complexity: Medium
Angel/Archangel to call upon: Not required

Transitions; The transition from spirit form into physical (birth) or the transition from the physical form to the spirit form (death). If the transition from one form to another did not go smoothly there may be healing required.

Preferred method: First, ask Archangel Nepum to identify all unhealthy transitions for the individual. Command, "I hereby command all transitions identified by Archangel Nepum to be fully healed in all timelines, dimensions, and realities. By my will, so it is."
Spiritual complexity: Medium
Angel/Archangel to call upon: Archangel Nepum

Auric Field and Chakras; Your aura is the energy field surrounding the body. It shows the overall health of our being. It serves two main purposes: to protect us, and to help us "feel" and be aware of our surroundings. From everyday living, it can become damaged, torn, or unhealthy.

Our chakras are centers of our body in which energy flows. There are seven major chakras and many minor chakras throughout the body. They can become unhealthy, "dirty," or not flowing in a healthy manner.

Having unhealthy chakras and/or an auric field can affect our everyday lives depending on its severity.

Preferred method: Reiki or Bio-Energy
Spiritual complexity: Medium → High
Angel/Archangel to call upon: Chakra Angel

Past Lives; Most souls have incarnated either on this planet or another planet in this Universe. Sometimes major events from past lives can affect us during this lifetime. Certain aspects of these events can "stick" with us and be detrimental to our evolution and quality of life.

Preferred method: Past-life Regression Therapy by a trained professional.
Spiritual complexity: Medium → High
Angel/Archangel to call upon: Call upon Angels/Archangels depending on what surfaces.

Unforgiveness; When a person or circumstance harms an individual, they can store it in their being as unforgiveness. This can severely impede the soul's evolution. Unforgiveness can be from this lifetime or a past life.

Preferred method: Identify the person or circumstance that needs to be forgiven. Say with as much sincerity as possible, "I forgive you," focusing on that person or circumstance. Repeat until there is no emotional charge towards that person or circumstance. Then say, "I forgive myself." Repeat until there is no emotional charge towards yourself.

Spiritual complexity: Medium → High

Angel/Archangel to call upon: Angel Esh

<u>**Unhealthy Beliefs**</u>**;** Any mindset that does not serve our highest and greatest good. This can be a belief carried from a previous lifetime or a belief learned in the current life.

Preferred method: Energy work such as Reiki on the head, Reiki bars and/or Belief Re-patterning.

Spiritual complexity: High

Angel/Archangel to call upon: Ask for assistance from the Philosophy Archangel (this Archangel has no name).

<u>**Traumas**</u>**;** Traumas tend to be multi-faceted and they are stored in our physical being. Ask Archangel Rageal to identify the traumas/events that need to be cleared. The details of the trauma are not required to be cleared.

Preferred method: Reiki and Command, "I hereby transmute all traumas in all timelines, dimensions, and realities. By my will, so it is."

Spiritual complexity: High

Angel/Archangel to call upon: Archangel Rageal

<u>**Contracts, Deals, and Agreements**</u>**;** Created between multiple parties, but one can also create contracts, deals, and agreements with one's self. Examples: vows or powerfully worded and intentional decisions. Many are created prior to incarnating, fewer are created

while incarnated. They can be carried over from past lives if they are not fulfilled.

Preferred method: Akashic Records clearing. Requires training.
Spiritual complexity: High → Advanced
Angel/Archangel to call upon: Lord of the Akashic Records

Spiritual Parasites; Tiny non-physical organisms that influence the overall health of the individual. They DO NOT feed off people. They DO affect aspects of the individual's Physical Being, such as their immune system. They can also affect the Emotional Being.

Preferred method: Must call upon an Archangel.
Spiritual complexity: Advanced
Angel/Archangel to call upon: Archangel Rageal

Curses and Hexes; Intentional and explicit harm desired upon another without physical contact.

Preferred method: Must call upon an angel.
Spiritual complexity: Advanced
Angel/Archangel to call upon: Angel Ntwoyn

Soul Retrieval; There are times in our lives, in this lifetime or a past one, when we can have such a major traumatic event that our soul can become splintered or scattered into different dimensions. It could be a spiritual trauma or a physical trauma, such as a car accident.

Preferred method: Soul retrieval by a Master Shaman or someone who specializes in this modality.
Spiritual complexity: Advanced
Angel/Archangel to call upon: Archangel Arkapa

After about a year, I was directed to start 'commanding' the changes to take place. This meant not doing energy work with my hands so often. Instead, I was to use the power of my voice, my emotions, and the power of my mind, body, and spirit to enforce change. This also required practice. All aspects of me had to be fully in alignment, and I had to reach a certain point in my healing process. I needed to be centered and grounded always, which is not as simple as it sounds.

After nearly a year and a half of preparation, and working together with Ken, Razial was satisfied Ken and I were ready to take our spiritual healing sessions into group settings.

The first group consisted of twenty-six people! I wondered if I could do for them the same as I could do for one individual. With much trepidation, I followed the guidance provided, hoping for the best.

Well, I need not have worried. The feedback provided by the group told me that they received a great deal of healing. Ever since, every one of our workshops has been at full capacity.

During our most recent session, Ken was told to tell me to command 'an increase in everyone's capacity to love.' This was an unusual request, and one they had never asked me to do before. I had no idea what to expect but I did as they asked. The group loved it! I asked them what had happened and they told me they felt a warm breeze come over them, felt to their core. Some people felt a tingling sensation. One woman made me laugh when she said she was changing her title from lightworker to loveworker. Commonly people say they come into the workshop with aches and pains, which are often gone by the end of the hour.

And so began, "Infinity Healing." Where we go from here is anyone's guess.

CHAPTER 22

——————◆——————

Energy Protection

In my first year of awakening, one of my biggest challenges was protection from lower energy. If affected, I would be tired, lethargic, grumpy, foggy, and occasionally I would get a mild headache. I had tried all the recommended solutions to protect myself, but to no avail. Surround yourself in white light, I was told. Nope, didn't work. You must carry protection crystals, I was told. This worked a little if I was carrying a crystal that absorbed the energy. The issue was that they needed to be cleared, which at the time I didn't know how to do. Their suggestions required concentration or maintenance. I found one oil blend that helped for a couple of hours but it wore off quickly and was only available if ordered from another country.

There was nothing that worked to my satisfaction. I felt there should be a tool that was simple and easy to use. How could I raise my vibration if I was constantly being dragged down? I knew this was a constant complaint from others as well. Empaths frequently expressed their challenges with lack of protection. So finally, I asked for an archangel to provide us with a formula for a better essential oil blend that we could use as a tool.

I received the list of ingredients and was told to give it to my friend Liane Pinel who has been professionally certified to work with essential oils. The formula of 13 essential oils had to be precise. I dug deep into my pocketbook to provide the funds needed to buy the expensive oils. I trusted the archangel who offered to help and I knew it was an investment worth making.

> The 13 oils we purchased were: Bergamot, Myrrh, Rosewood, Ylang Ylang, Rose (Bulgarian), Melissa Leaf, Black Pepper, Litsea Cubeba, Arborvitae (Wild), Cedarwood (Atlas and Alantic), Peppermint.

> Spiritually blended and energetically charged with the Empath symbol vibration, this 100 percent pure essential oil blend was bottled. We chose a sweet almond carrier oil for the smaller bottles and a floral water base for the larger bottles.

The scent was beautiful! Truly created by the angels. Completely unisex, it was quickly appreciated by men and women alike. Since it has no perfumes or fragrances, the scent dissipates but it was never meant to be used as a perfume anyway. It is the protection that really matters. If you want to make the scent last longer, then use a lava bead(s) which absorbs the oil which you can wear in a bracelet or necklace.

The instructions were clear and simple. Put the essential oil blend on the inside crook of the arm, back of the neck or wherever you are guided first thing in the morning, and reapply halfway through the day or as needed. Every five hours is ideal.

The oil combines with the essence of the individual, creating a temporary protective barrier. It also clears away any existing lower energy and other people's energy instantly!

The Energy Protection Blend was released to the public on August 13, 2017 and it has already helped so many people, including my partner, Ken. The feedback has been so positive. We are blessed to have been given this gift and I will continue to do my part in making it available to those who need it.

I will share one testimonial that touched me deeply. It came from one of my regular clients.

"One of my workmates suffers from anxiety attacks and depression. Medication doesn't always work and has troublesome side effects. She was having a particularly bad event yesterday and I had my Energy Protection oil roll-on applicator in my purse. I asked her if she'd like to try it. She accepted. Half an hour later, she's telling me she feels so much better; very calm. Today, she told me she had the most restful sleep ever. I did not discuss any possible effects with her, prior to her using it. This protection oil is amazing!"

For order information, please refer to the back of this book.

CHAPTER 23

─────────◆──────✦──────◆─────────

Not Goodbye

You may notice that my writing style and tone has changed significantly since my first book. I noticed too. It's a true reflection of the evolution I have undergone since my awakening.

I have changed physically as well. My bones and facial structure are different as you might be able to tell from my author photos. People close to me like my son and close friends have commented on the changes in my features. Since puberty I have always struggled with acne. Recently that has cleared up and even some of my wrinkles are disappearing making it seem like I have somehow reversed some of my aging process. For most of my life I would hide behind my long hair when my low self-esteem would rear its ugly head. In phases, I kept cutting my hair shorter and shorter. I have since cut my long hair off entirely, in place of a short hairstyle. My demeanor is calmer and more reflective. I don't react or get triggered as easily, if at all. Spiritually I have developed abilities I never knew were possible.

No doubt I am not the same person I once was. In a year from now I may not be the same person I am now. I hope I am not, as it means I am continuing to evolve back into my true nature and form.

I have bared my soul to you my readers, once again, by sharing my very personal journey in the hopes that I guide your awakening and assist you on your own path. I hope you will use the tools and tips I have provided to heal and bring light to yourself and others. My only goal, or agenda if you will, is to make this world a better place.

I am still seeking answers to questions I have not even thought of yet. Every day I learn something new. Each new day brings wonder and another piece to the puzzle. As I learn, I share. I have no desire to hold all the answers inside. I will share each new insight as I find it. You will still have to find your own way, your own path and make your own choices.

It's interesting to note I am finishing my second book on the anniversary of my third year of my awakening. Sept 6, 2017 marks three years since my spiritual journey began. I am coming from a better, healthier place now. My personal healing has brought me to a place of peace and understanding. Each day my abilities grow or maybe they are simply becoming more accessible as I clear away the cobwebs and everything that was blocking them. Shifts and changes still sneak up on me regularly.

I do not know what comes next. Slowly, but surely, I am making myself available to others for the opportunity to offer healing, guidance, and love. I believe I will continue to teach workshops, which I enjoy immensely. I hope there will be many author signing events in my future. Of greater importance though, is the Infinity Healing that Ken and I offer together. It is only through healing that our true selves can shine through.

There will be a third book on the horizon, though whether it belongs to this series or is about an entirely new subject, I do not know yet. I am sure I will be equally as surprised as you by what I channel with my automatic writing.

Thank you, dear readers, for choosing to read my book.

PS. I am adding a bonus chapter! My most popular and most frequently requested meditation that I combine with the use of my crystal singing bowl. Please use freely if you offer meditation classes for others.

BONUS CHAPTER KIM'S SOUND HEALING MEDITATION

Today we are starting our meditation with the healing sounds of a crystal singing bowl. As you listen to the beautiful tones, allow the crystal waves to wash over you and imagine your body getting lighter and lighter with every note. Starting at your head and working your way down to your feet you will become weightless. It will feel as if your spirit is lifting out of your body, but of course you are always tethered to your body. Release any tension. Let go of all anxiety. Discharge lower energy through your hands and the bottoms of your feet. Breathe out your fears and breathe in love. Liberate your being.

Play Crystal Singing Bowl for 1-2 min

Now you are completely weightless. All tension has been released and you are beginning to float like a balloon. You are warm and safe and floating gently with the breeze. It feels so good to just relax and be carried as if you were on a cloud. This is your moment to be present. To your right, you see a rainbow. You gaze at the rainbow in the sky and marvel at this magnificent creation. As you observe its vibrant colors, all the colors of the rainbow start to swirl and blend together, mixing until they become pure white. This pure white color becomes a white light.

Move closer and surround yourself in this white light and draw it into you. Your body fills with pure, warm, loving, white light. As you draw in this pure energy you get even lighter than before. It's as if this white light is hugging you inside and out with so much love. Filling you with love. Use this light to transmute any lower energy or blockages from your chakras. See this white light dissolving anything that is not in your highest and greatest good. Let this white light melt away your burdens.

Take a moment now to invite your guides to be with you during this meditation. Give them permission to be with you. Know they are there, even if you cannot see them. Maybe you can sense their presence. They love you so much. Send them love and gratitude for they have always been there for you.

Now you are ready to reach a higher consciousness. With nothing holding you back, you start to rise as if you were filled with helium. Through the clouds, you rise. There is no discomfort and you are completely safe. You continue rising. The stars are all around you, lighting your way, and you keep lifting higher and higher. You pass through an invisible barrier with ease. You have done this before and you are excited to be doing it again with intention. You know the way.

In this state, you remember you can have wings. You feel them expand from your back and open wide. It feels so good to stretch your wings open. You can fly from here and you start to ascend in flight. Your wings carry you high and you pass through the next invisible barrier.

As you reach higher levels of consciousness you feel your mind, body, and spirit start to heal from the love that surrounds you. The vibration of your entire being is raised just by being here. You bask in the higher vibrations and allow your being to be lifted, healed, and loved. How you feel now is etched into your memory and you know you will be able to come back here again and again. Your guides are nearby if you need them. If you feel tingly, just remain still and allow the waves of pure energy to wash over you and heal you. You can use your senses to observe your surroundings. What do you hear? What do you feel? What do you see with your mind's eye? If nothing, that's okay. Know that your vibration is being raised simply by being here. Your guides watch over you as you bask in these higher vibrations.

If you feel you need to reach a higher level of consciousness and vibration just open your wings and continue up through the next invisible barrier. If you feel that you are getting lightheaded do not go any higher. You can always come back down until you feel more comfortable. Each time you do this meditation your body will adjust to these new vibrations; you will be able to go higher next time if you choose. There is no hurry. Today we seek only love and healing. Your mind is clear and open. Just experience this moment without judgement or analysis. There is time for that later. Take a deep breath. Absorb these new fantastic vibrations of the Universe into your entire self. Maybe there is a message for you. If there is no message today, there might be a message next time. Messages may come in many forms. A word, a symbol, a name, a picture, a feeling, a sensation. If today there is a message, welcome it with gratitude. You won't always get a message and that's okay. This moment is for you and that's enough.

It's time to bring this higher vibration back to our bodies. You can bring back any messages you received. Slowly start to descend, back the way you came through the invisible barriers. As you come back, your wings fold up and disappear. You feel that you are getting closer to your body. Past the stars that lit your way. You start to regain some of your density. Through the clouds. The white light reforms back into a beautiful rainbow. Thank your loving guides for being on this journey with you and watching over you. As you start to integrate back into your body, allow the sounds of the singing bowl to bring you to full awareness. As you listen to the musical notes, wiggle your fingers and toes and stretch your body. Inhale and exhale deep and long.

Play Singing Bowl for 1-2 min

Let's take a moment to ground our energies. Imagine a cord extending from your root chakra and going down into the earth. Deep into the earth, through the dirt, the rocks, the water until you get to the center of the Earth. Now wrap that cord around the center of the Earth a few times. Once securely anchored the cord will work its way back up through the Earth back to your root chakra, bringing all that grounding from Mother Earth to your root chakra. Inhale and exhale deep and long.

Now wrap your arms around yourself and say, "I love you."

Love and Light my friends.

ABOUT THE AUTHOR

Photographer: Rosealee Lagace of RMLFoto

Kim Wuirch is an Empath, Spiritual Healer, and Archangel communicator, who works with people of all ages, to assist with healing and spiritual growth.

Kim knows that people are being awakened in waves across the world. She wants them to know they are not alone and they are not crazy. To do this she shares her journey.

After Kim's first book launched, *Waking Up An Empath, A Year in The Life of a Empath From Awakening to Spiritual Healer*, the spiritual community began talking about Kim and seeking her out for spiritual healing and training.

Kim has progressed from learning many existing spiritual modalities to forging her own path and methods of spiritual healing. Kim has brought the world the Empath Symbol, Infinity Healing, and her Energy Protection Oil.

To see her blog and website, go to: www.KimWuirch.com

ENERGY PROTECTION BLEND

Use this oil blend daily, whether you are leaving the house or not. It is recommended that you make a practice of using it as soon as you get up in the morning and reapply as needed throughout the day as it will dissipate (approximately every five hours). If you forget, no problem! It will clear lower energy the instant it is applied.

Tip Dropper Glass Bottle with Essential oils (Sweet Almond Oil Base)	5ml
Roll-on Glass Bottle with metal rollerball Essential oils (Sweet Almond Oil Base)	10ml
Fine Mist Glass Spray Bottle (Floral water base)	2oz
Fine Mist Glass Spray Bottle (Floral water base) (comes with bonus gold colored travel refillable atomizer)	4oz

5ml and 10ml bottles contains: Sweet Almond oil base with; Bergamot, Myrrh, Rosewood, Ylang Ylang, Rose (Bulgarian), Melissa Leaf, Black Pepper, Litsea Cubeba, Arborvitae (Wild), Cedarwood (Atlas and Alantic), Peppermint.

2oz and 4oz bottles contains: Floral and Spring Waters with; Bergamot, Myrrh, Rosewood, Ylang Ylang, Rose (Bulgarian), Melissa Leaf, Black Pepper, Litsea Cubeba, Arborvitae (Wild), Cedarwood (Atlas and Alantic), Peppermint.

Professionally blended and energetically charged. 100% Pure Essential Oil Blend. Therapeutic Quality. For External Use Only!

All of Kim's products are available on the following website www. KimWuirch.com

OTHER SERVICES

Infinity Healing

To inquire about booking an Infinity Healing group session for a corporate or private event, contact Kim Wuirch through her website at www.KimWuirch.com

Workshops and Training

Kim and her partner Ken offer a range of workshops, including but not limited to:
Usui Reiki Level1/2 and Usui Reiki 3/Master
Akashic Records Beginner, Intermediate, and Advanced
Channeling
Empath Development
Angels and Archangels
and many more…

Media

Radio: Kim has been on HayHouse radio with author Gerry Gavin (Gavin, 2012), Blog Talk Radio Best Life Café with author Cathy Anello (Anello, 2016), as well as other various blog talk radio shows.

TV: Kim currently co-hosts a TV show on a TV station in Alberta called CATV1 (available online).

Kim was also interviewed on WBBZ TV Buffalo's Buzz in Buffalo, New York.

<u>Newspapers:</u> Kim has been featured in an article for *The Buffalo News*, Refresh section, *The Airdrie Echo,* and in *Airdrie City View* newspapers.

Follow Kim's upcoming media appearances at: <u>www.kimwuirch.com/media</u>

Presentations

Kim is available for presentations not only about her book but about any of the spiritual topics discussed in her books, blogs, or that she offers in her workshops and training.

Author Signings

Kim is available for author signings at any of the stores that carry her book. Kim has provided many author signings at bookstores such as Indigo/Chapters and Barnes and Noble, as well as many independent metaphysical, health food stores, and libraries.

QR CODE

#WakingUpAnEmpath
#AwakenedEmpath

REFERENCES

Anello, C. (2016). *Six Months to Live.* Balboa Press.

Gavin, G. (2012). *Messages from Margaret.* Hayhouse UK.

Harrison, S. B. (2002). *Past Lives, Future Healing.* NAL; Reprint edition.

John of God. (2017, August 30). Retrieved from http://www.johnofgod-brazil.net/

Pinel, L. (2017). The Unveiling of a Crystal - When Humanity Needs It the Most. Airdrie, Alberta, Canada.

Rockwell, A. s. (1984). Somebody's Watching Me.

Walsch, N. D. (2017). *Conversations with God; Book 4; Awaken the Species.* Rainbow Ridge Books, LLC.

Wuirch, K. (2016, 12 28). *Waking Up An Empath.* Balboa Press.

Zialcita, T. (2013). *Universal Conscious Self - simple steps to connect to your true essence.* Balboa Press.

INDEX